How to Fix your PC Problems

D0682688

Robert Penfold

Bernard Babani (publishing) Ltd
The Grampians
Shepherds Bush Road
London W6 7NF
England

www.babanibooks.com

Please note

Although every care has been taken with the production of this book to ensure that any projects, designs, modifications, and/or programs, etc., contained herewith, operate in a correct and safe manner and also that any components specified are normally available in Great Britain, the Publisher and Author do not accept responsibility in any way for the failure (including fault in design) of any projects, design, modification, or program to work correctly or to cause damage to any equipment that it may be connected to or used in conjunction with, or in respect of any other damage or injury that may be caused, nor do the Publishers accept responsibility in any way for the failure to obtain specified components.

Notice is also given that if any equipment that is still under warranty is modified in any way or used or connected with home-built equipment then that warranty may be void.

© 2009 BERNARD BABANI (publishing) LTD

First Published - May 2009

British Library Cataloguing in Publication Data
A catalogue record for this book is available from the British Library

ISBN   978 0 85934 705 1

Cover Design by Gregor Arthur
Printed and bound in Great Britain for Bernard Babani (publishing) Ltd

In an ideal world you would set up a new PC to suit your requirements and then go on using it in trouble-free fashion for many years. Unfortunately, the realities of modern computing are rather different to the ideal. Most modern PCs tend to evolve over a period of time, with new software being installed, and probably new hardware and peripheral gadgets being added as well. The operating system has to change to accommodate this evolution, but each change has the potential for introducing problems. Sometimes the system seems to run into problems for no apparent reason, but the cause is probably an automatic update or an earlier change that has taken a while to produce any noticeable hitches. If Windows should cease working properly it is not usually too difficult to get it up and running again. Most faults introduced into the system are easily reversed, provided you know how. This book details some simple procedures that enable many common Windows and general PC faults to be quickly pinpointed and rectified.

The first chapter deals with what almost certainly qualifies as the most common Windows problem, which is a gradual slowing down of the system over a period of time. Some simple measures are usually sufficient to reverse this problem, and if used right from the start will prevent the system from going into decline in the first place. Chapter two deals with other common Windows and PC problems, such as difficulties when starting up or shutting down the computer, using the System Restore facility to reverse practically any damage to the operating system, and running old software on a new PC. The final chapter deals with common problems when connecting the computer to the outside world, such as curing printer problems, clearing a blocked Internet connection, and getting the fastest possible download speed.

This book is written in plain English and, wherever possible, avoids technical jargon. Little previous knowledge of computing is assumed, but in some sections it will be helpful if the reader knows the basic fundamentals of using a PC and the Windows Vista operating system. It is certainly not necessary to be a computer expert in order to use the methods featured here. Obviously due care needs to be taken when dealing with the operating system, but the built-in Windows tools are safe provided a bit of common sense is exercised when using them. The same is true of most third-party utility software such as tuning utilities.

Much of the book also applies to Windows XP machines, but bear in mind that there are often minor differences in the way a given feature operates in XP and Vista.

Robert Penfold

Trademarks

Microsoft, Windows, Windows XP, and Windows Vista are either registered trademarks or trademarks of Microsoft Corporation.

All other brand and product names used in this book are recognised trademarks, or registered trademarks of their respective companies. There is no intent to use any trademarks generically and readers should investigate ownership of a trademark before using it for any purpose.

Contents

1

When things slow down 1

Please note

Undertaking tasks such as changing video settings of your computer, deleting unwanted files, uninstalling software, and defragmenting a hard disc drive should not invalidate the manufacturer's warranty. Neither should using software that helps with general maintenance of the computer, such as tuning utilities and diagnostics software. Directly tinkering with the operating system, such as making changes to the Windows Registry should not normally invalidate any warranties, and should not damage the hardware. However, it could render the operating system unusable, leaving the computer out of commission. It would then be the responsibility of the user to restore the operating system to a usable state. Making direct changes to the Windows Registry is a topic that is not covered in this book, and it is something that should only be undertaken by those with the necessary experience and knowledge to sort out any problems that arise.

Adding new hardware inside a PC, such as adding memory modules, does often invalidate the manufacturer's warranty. It does not affect your statutory rights though, provided any additions made to the computer do not cause any damage. Changing settings so that the hardware operates beyond its normal parameters (over-clocking) can damage the hardware, will almost certainly invalidate the computer manufacturer's guarantee, and probably leave you very much on your own if things go awry. Over-clocking is not a subject that is included in this book.

Further, you are advised to check the Terms and Conditions of your own particular hardware and software warranties and, also, those of any equipment maintenance agreements that you might have.

When things slow down

Efficient files

On the face of it, once your PC is set up correctly there should be nothing more to do. Surely it will go on operating efficiently for many years without you having to do anything more. Practical experience suggests that this is pure fantasy for most users, and that it is quite normal for a PC to run noticeably slower after it has been in use for a few months. In fact it can noticeably slow down in the space of a few weeks.

So why does a PC tend to slow down over a period of time, and what can you do to rectify matters? The fall-off in performance is usually due to the hard disc drive taking longer to load files into memory, but the problem is not really caused by the hardware. A PC's hardware normally works at full tilt or not at all. The problem has more to do with the number of files on the hard disc drive. Most people add more programs and data to their PCs over a period of time. Each program that is added tends to make the Windows Registry grow ever bigger, and the newly added files tend to be spread all over the hard disc rather than grouped neatly together. Getting a PC to run efficiently therefore consists largely of removing unnecessary files and keeping the remaining files organised properly on the hard disc drive.

Hidden tools

There are numerous utility programs available that help to get a PC working efficiently and keep it that way, and it is easy to spend a lot of money on PC utility software. However, these programs are not essential, and it would be a mistake to overlook the built-in tools of Windows itself. It would be a mistake, but it would also be quite easy because they are buried quite deep in the menu structure. From the start menu select All Programs, Accessories, System Tools, and then the required program.

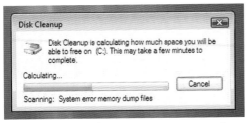

Fig.1.1 The Disk Cleanup program scans the disc for unnecessary files

A good one to start with is Disk Cleanup. The Disk Cleanup program used in this example is the one in Windows Vista, but essentially the same facility is available in Windows XP.

As its name suggests, Disk Cleanup looks for unnecessary files on the selected disc drive. With a multi-user PC you will be asked if you wish to clean only your own files or those of all users. By its very nature the Disk Cleanup program is unlikely to remove anything of significance, but it is still advisable to clean only your own files. Of course, this will reduce the number of unnecessary files that are removed, and ideally all users should periodically use this program. You must be using an account with administrator status in order to use the program with files other than your own.

There will probably be another pop-up window where Windows asks your permission to proceed, and this is a standard Windows Vista security measure. At least one of these windows will pop-up when you try to make practically any changes to the system, and it is impossible to proceed unless you indicate that you wish to continue. No mention of these pop-up security messages will be made elsewhere in this book, but they will be encountered when following many of the examples provided throughout this publication. Simply indicate that you wish to proceed whenever one of them pops up.

The window of Figure 1.1 appears when the Disk Cleanup program is finally launched, and this indicates that the program is scanning the hard disc for files that it thinks are no longer required. With a computer that has more than one hard disc drive you might have to select the disc to be processed before the scanning process is commenced. Either way, a summary of the program's findings will eventually be displayed (Figure 1.2), but with large drives containing a huge number of files it can take a few minutes for this window to appear. It is not possible to select files for deletion on an individual basis, and there will usually be far too many of them for this to be a practical proposition. Instead, you are presented with various file categories, and all the files in a category can be erased by first ticking the corresponding checkbox. The OK button is operated once all the categories for deletion have been selected.

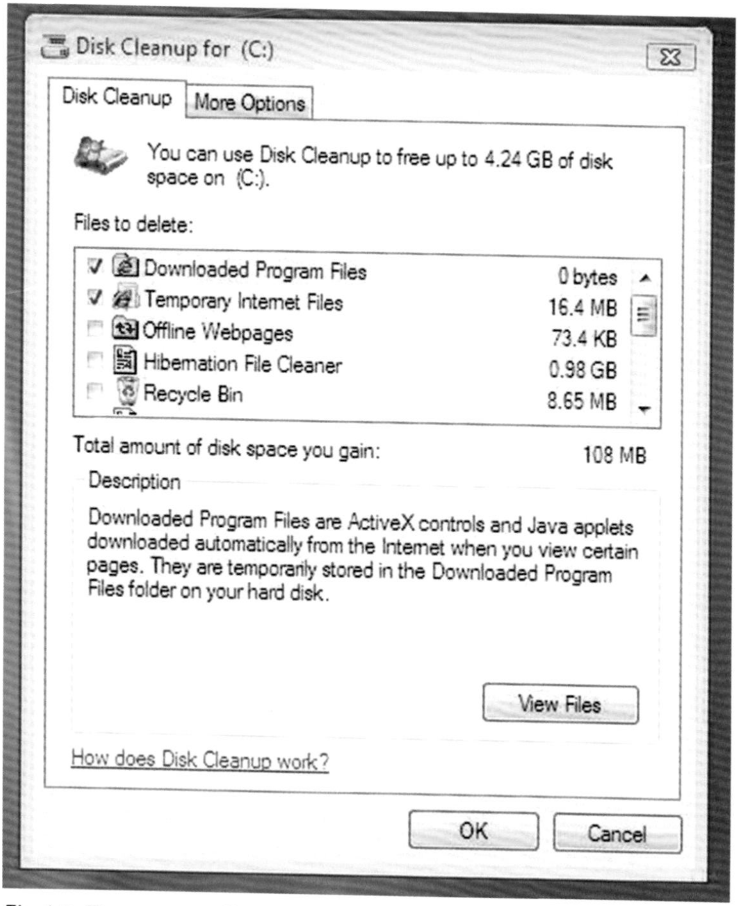

Fig.1.2 *The program lists the non-essential files that it has located*

The Temporary Internet Files are copies of the files downloaded when viewing Internet pages. These are stored on the hard disc in order to speed up access if you go back to the same page. Rather than downloading the page again, the copy stored on the disc is used. Of course, this only works if the page has not changed since your last visit, or most of the files used in the page are the same. It is otherwise necessary for the page to be downloaded again, and a copy of the new page is stored in the cache on the hard disc. This leads to a gradual

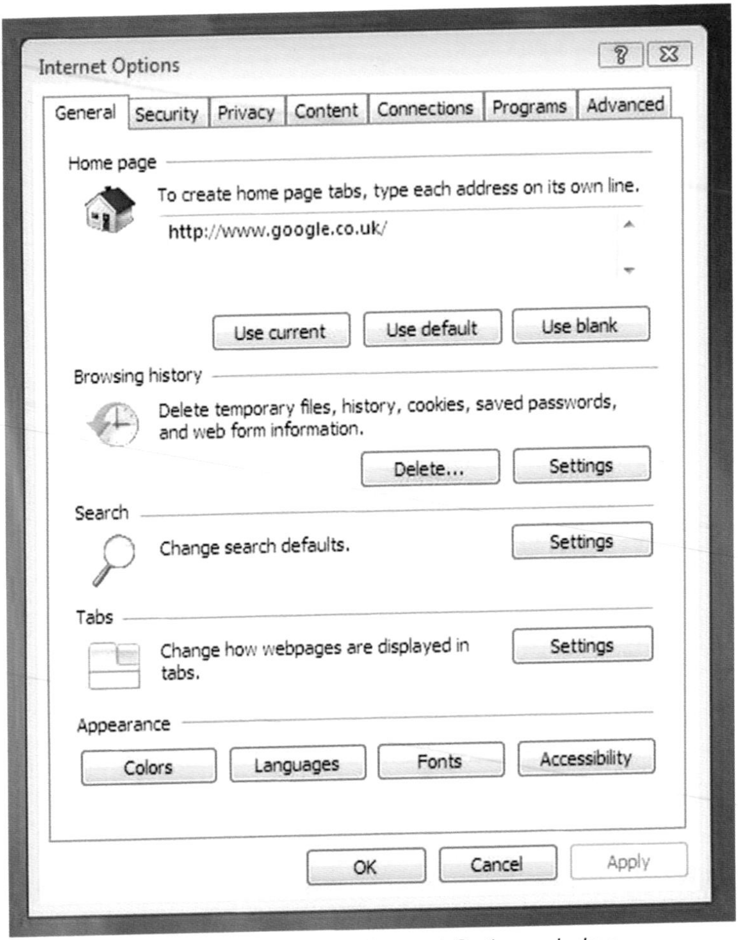

Fig.1.3 *The General section of the Internet Options window*

build-up of files on the hard disc, especially if you do research on the Internet and visit dozens of sites.

The files are not stored indefinitely on the disc, and Windows automatically deletes the oldest files once a certain amount of disc space has been used. It is easy to alter the maximum amount of disc space that is used for this temporary storage. Start by going into Internet Explorer and then select Internet Options from the Tools menu. This produces a

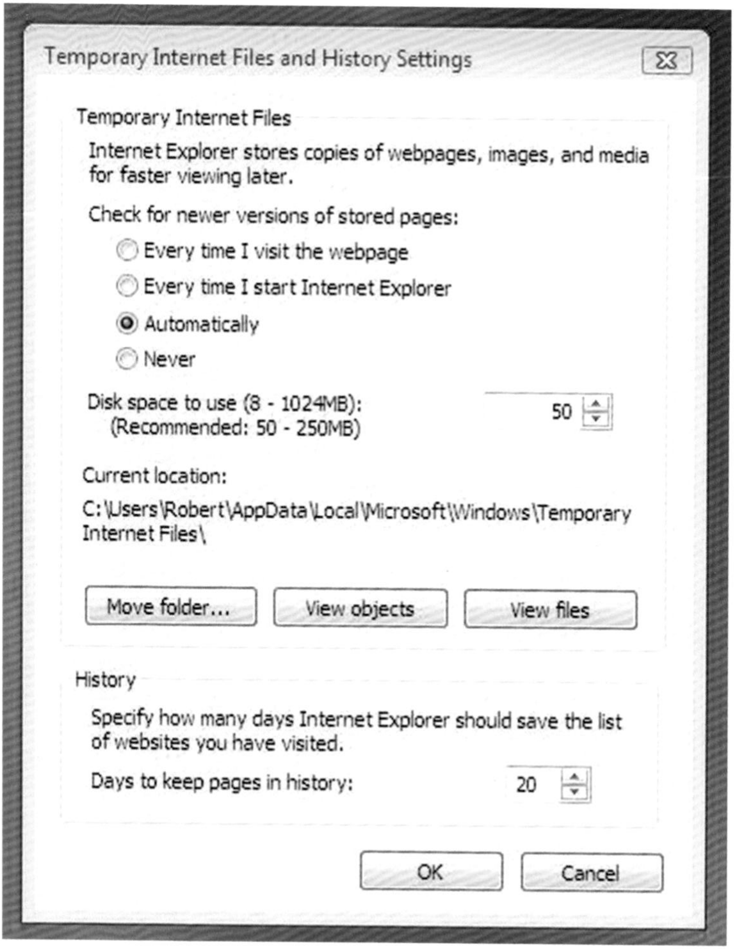

Temporary Internet Files and History Settings   ⊠

Temporary Internet Files

Internet Explorer stores copies of webpages, images, and media for faster viewing later.

Check for newer versions of stored pages:

○ Every time I visit the webpage

○ Every time I start Internet Explorer

◉ Automatically

○ Never

Disk space to use (8 - 1024MB):   50 ⇅
(Recommended: 50 - 250MB)

Current location:

C:\Users\Robert\AppData\Local\Microsoft\Windows\Temporary Internet Files\

[Move folder...]   [View objects]   [View files]

History

Specify how many days Internet Explorer should save the list of websites you have visited.

Days to keep pages in history: 20 ⇅

[OK]   [Cancel]

Fig.1.4 This window can be used to alter the maximum amount of disc space used for temporary Internet files

window like the one in Figure 1.3. The General tab will probably be selected by default, but if necessary select it manually.

The temporary Internet files can be erased by operating the Delete button near the middle of the window. To alter the maximum amount of space used for these temporary files, operate the Settings button just to the right of the Delete button, which will produce the window of Figure 1.4.

Enter the required size in the middle right-hand section of the window, or use the up and down arrow buttons to set the required cache size. The figure in the textbox is the size of the cache in megabytes, and 50 megabytes should be perfectly adequate for most users. To make this change take effect and move things back to the Internet Properties window, operate the OK button in this window in order to close it. Then operate the OK button in the Internet Properties window in order to close it.

Cache size

Is it worth reducing the size of the cache for temporary Internet files and deleting its contents from time to time? This really depends on the setup you are using and the way in which it is used. With a broadband Internet connection the caching system does not necessarily bring great benefits, since most pages will probably download quite fast. It will only be of real help when downloading pages that contain large files or accessing sites that are stored on slow or very busy servers. When using an ordinary dialup connection the benefits of caching are likely to be much greater. Of course, caching is ineffective with any system if you do not keep going back to the same old web pages, or you do but there are substantial changes each time you visit them.

In practice, and regardless of the theory, the caching system does seem to be ineffective when you have a cache that occupies hundreds of megabytes or more of hard disc space, and what is likely to be tens of thousands of files. If you use Windows Explorer to go into the Temporary Internet folder it could well take the program half a minute to produce a list of all the files, and the number of files could well be in excess of 50 thousand. This gives a hint as to why the caching system can become inefficient.

If you find that your Internet connection is generally working well, but certain sites that are normally quite fast are proving to be very slow and difficult to access, removing the temporary Internet files will sometimes cure the problem. Presumably something has gone awry with the caching system, and clearing the cache removes the files that are causing the problem.

A large cache of temporary Internet files can be particularly inefficient if there is a lack of vacant hard disc space. Allocating a large amount of space for temporary Internet storage could greatly reduce the amount of disc space left for other forms of temporary storage, causing a significant reduction in the overall performance of the PC. If spare hard disc space is strictly limited it is definitely a good idea to reduce the amount of space allocated to storing temporary Internet files.

Having erased the temporary Internet cache it is likely that Internet access will be a bit slower initially when using your favourite sites. This will be especially noticeable with slow sites or when using a dialup connection. However, the cached files will be reinstated after visiting each of these sites for the first time, so any slowdown will only be temporary.

Temporary files

Returning briefly to the categories of files listed by the Disk Cleanup program, the Temporary Files category contains files that have been placed in a "TEMP" folder by applications programs. Many applications generate temporary files that are normally erased when the program is closed. However, some of these files get left behind, possibly due to a program shutting down abnormally. Some programs are not designed quite as well as they might be and habitually leave temporary files on the hard disc drive. The files included in this category are temporary types that are more than one week old, and it should be safe to delete them. Doing so is unlikely to free much hard disc space though.

Recycle Bin

As most Windows users are no doubt aware, when you delete files they are not deleted immediately but are instead placed in the Recycle Bin. The Recycle Bin is just a folder on the hard drive, but it is one that is normally handled by Windows or indirectly by the user. Of course, Windows does not continue storing deleted files indefinitely. There is an upper limit to the size of the Recycle Bin, and eventually old deleted files will be completely removed in order to make space for newer ones.

The default size for the Recycle Bin is quite large, so a substantial number of files can be amassed over a period of time. It can be altered by right-clicking on the Recycle Bin icon and selecting Properties from the pop-up menu. This produces the window of Figure 1.5, and the maximum size of the Recycle Bin can then be set by entering the appropriate figure into the textbox. With Windows XP and earlier versions of Windows, the figure set here is the percentage of the drive's full capacity that will be used for storing deleted files. With Windows Vista the figure in the textbox is the size of the Recycle Bin in megabytes. A gigabyte is equal to 1024 megabytes incidentally.

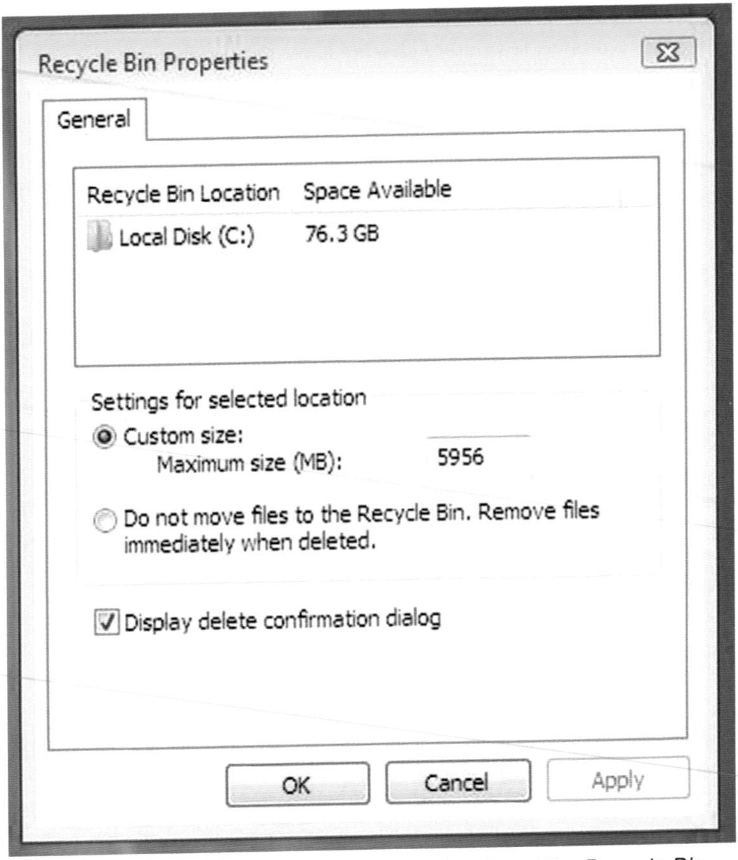

Fig.1.5 This window can be used to alter the size of the Recycle Bin

It is not necessary to utilise the Recycle Bin at all. It can be switched off by operating the appropriate radio button in the Recycle Bin Properties window. It is also possible to circumvent the Recycle Bin by selecting the files to be deleted, holding down the shift key, and then operating the Del key or selecting the Delete option from the appropriate menu. The usual warning message will still appear so that you have a chance to change your mind before the files are deleted. This message can be suppressed by ticking the checkbox near the bottom of the Recycle Bin Properties window.

When fully deleting files, whether via the Disk Cleanup program or by other means, bear in mind that Windows offers no way of retrieving files once they have been fully deleted. It is often possible to retrieve deleted files using an undelete utility, but there is no guarantee that this will be possible. It will certainly not be possible to retrieve a file once the disc space it occupied has been overwritten by another file. Even with a partially overwritten file there is little prospect of retrieving anything worthwhile. Using a Recycle Bin of modest size is a safer way of deleting files.

The other categories in the Disk Cleanup program tend to be those concerned with things such as diagnostics. These files are not necessarily of any use, but there will probably be little point in deleting them. The number of files and the disc space that they occupy will both be quite small, if there are actually any files at all.

Defragmenters

Many users tend to assume that files are automatically stored on the hard disc on the basis of one continuous section of disc per file. Unfortunately, it does not necessarily operate in this fashion. When Windows is first installed on a PC it is likely that files will be added in this manner. The applications programs are then installed, and things will probably continue in an organised fashion with files stored on the disc as single clumps of data. Even if things have progressed well thus far, matters soon take a turn for the worse when the user starts deleting files, adding new files or programs, deleting more files, and so on.

Gaps are produced in the continuous block of data when files are deleted. Windows utilises the gaps when new data is added, but it will use them even if each one is not large enough to take a complete file. If necessary, it will use dozens of these small vacant areas to accommodate a large file. This can result in a large file being spread across the disc in numerous tiny packets of data, which makes reading the file a relatively slow and inefficient business. The computer can seriously slow down when a substantial number of files get fragmented in this way.

There are programs called defragmenters that reorganise the files on a disc drive so that, as far as reasonably possible, large files are not fragmented. A program of this type is available in the System Tools submenu as the Disk Defragmenter. This utility has something of a chequered past, and in older versions of Windows it gave odd results with some disc drives. At some point in the proceedings the estimated

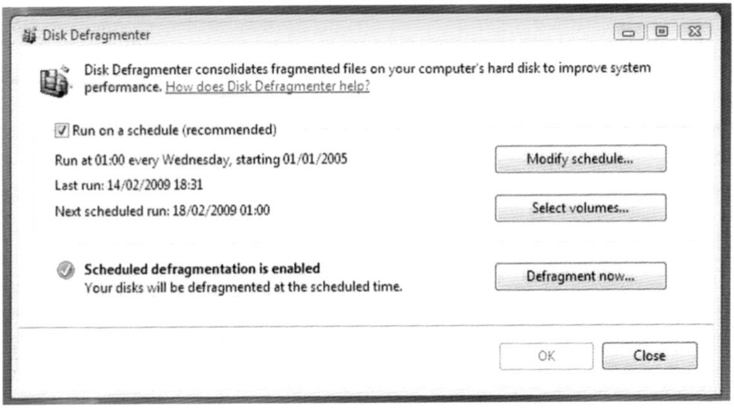

Fig.1.6 The initial window of the Disk Defragmenter program

time to completion would start to rise and usually kept rising with the process never finishing. Provided you are using a reasonably modern version of Windows there should be no problem of this type and the Disk Defragmenter program should work well. There should certainly be no problems with the versions included with Windows XP and Vista.

Launching the Vista defragmenter program produces a window like the one in Figure 1.6. Scheduled defragmenting will probably be used by default, and this has the advantage of keeping the hard disc drive running efficiently without any intervention by the user. You do not have to accept the default schedule, and operating the Modify Schedule button produces the control panel of Figure 1.7. The pop-down menu at the top provides a choice of daily, weekly, or monthly operation. Where weekly or monthly scheduling is selected, the other two menus enable the day and start time to be selected. Remove the tick from the checkbox in the main window if you do not wish to have the program run automatically.

In normal use the disc should not become fragmented so quickly that daily use of the defragmenter program is required. Weekly or even monthly use should suffice. The best time for scheduled use of the program is when there is a high likelihood of the computer being switched on, but little chance of it being used for any intensive computing. Running the defragmenter program will use some of the computer's processing power, and could result in application programs running noticeably slower than normal.

Whether or not scheduled operation has been selected, the program can be used at any time by operating the Defragment Now button. This

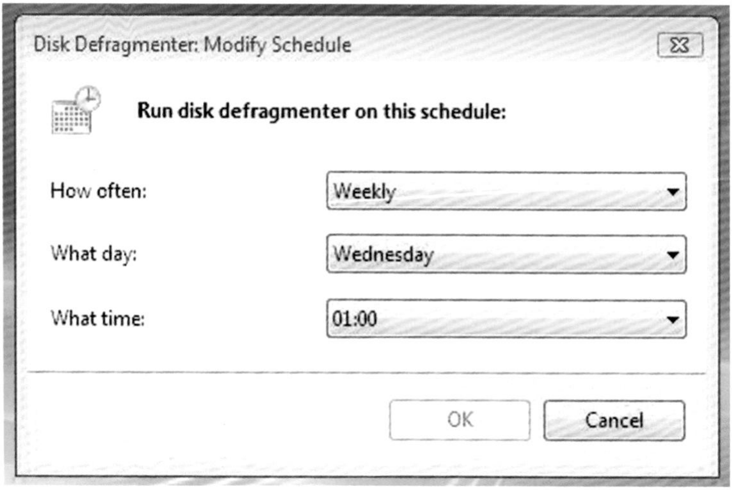

Fig.1.7 Regular operation of the program can be scheduled here

launches a small window where the hard drives to be processed can be selected. Of course, if there is only one drive, as in this example, this window is really superfluous. Operate the OK button to go ahead and process the selected drive or drives. The defragmentation process usually takes at least a few minutes, and with a large disc that is badly fragmented it can take several hours. The process can be halted at any time by operating the Cancel Defragmentation button, but ending the program prematurely could result in little or no improvement being obtained.

Disc problems

Problems with the hard disc drive can result in the computer slowing down as it has to reread parts of files in order to correct errors. However, a more common symptom of disc problems is the computer producing an error message indicating that it could not read the drive properly, or the computer simply crashing. There are actually two totally different types of problem with disc drives, and one of these is the hardware type. This can be due to something in the mechanism of the drive being slightly out of kilter, but a fault of this type usually develops quite rapidly into a total failure of the drive. Persistent problems with reading errors are more likely to be due to the magnetic coating on a small part of the disc being damaged or just of inadequate quality. There is a way around

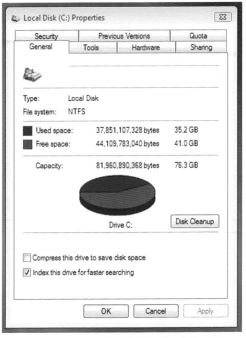

Fig.1.8 *The Properties window for Drive C*

this, which is to have the bad sections of the disc marked as such by the operating system, and removed from use.

The second type of disc problem is of the software variety, and with this type of fault there is nothing at all wrong with the drive itself. The problem is more to do with the disc filing system, and the way in which it stores the files on a disc. As already pointed out, files are not necessarily in large and continuous chunks of data on the disc. With a large file it is not unusual for there to be several sections in various places on the disc. This is fine provided the operating system knows where each piece is located so that it can load the pieces and put them together in the right order. There is usually no problem here, but things can occasionally go awry. Errors can occur for example, if the computer is switched off or crashes while data is being written to the disc.

It is usually possible for the disc filing system to be repaired so that the computer can operate normally thereafter. However, this is not to say that it will be possible to recover any damaged data. With this type of fault it is likely that some data was never actually written to the disc, or that some existing data will have been partially overwritten by other information. While it might be possible to recover some fragments of data, the chances of them being of any practical use are very slim. Be aware that bad sectors of the drive are also likely to produce some loss of data. Of course, at least one back-up copy should always be made of any important disc files.

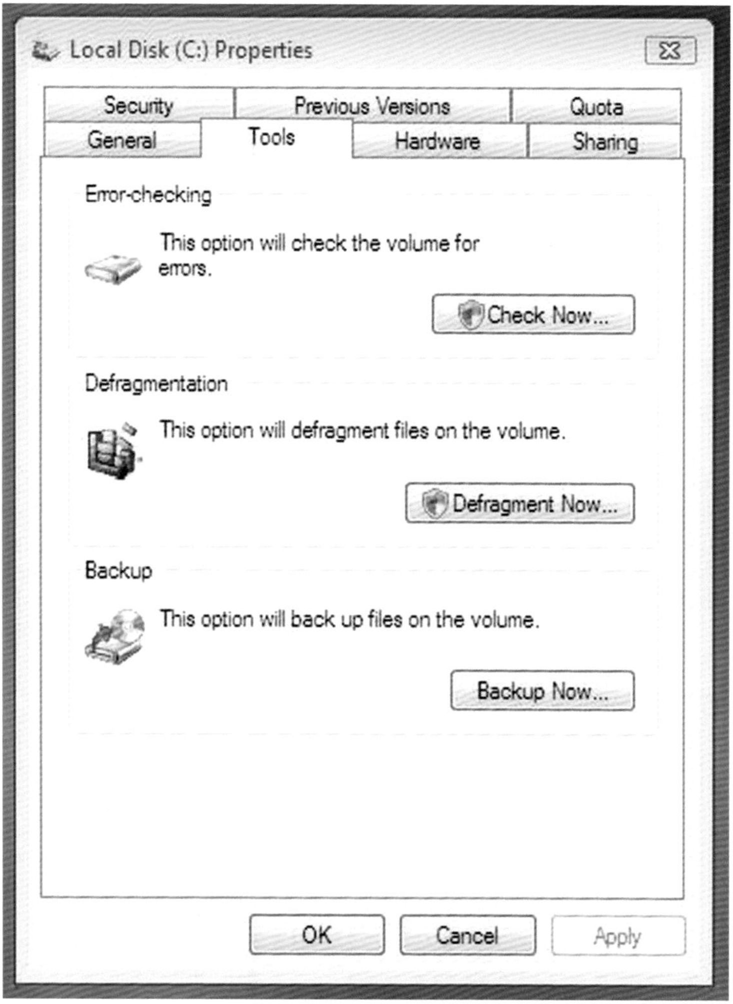

Fig.1.9 This windows provides access to the error checking facility

The built-in disc checking facilities of Windows have changed substantially over the years, but in Windows Vista it is the Check Disk program that is used to find and (possibly) repair hard disc problems. Essentially the same facility is available to users of Windows XP. This

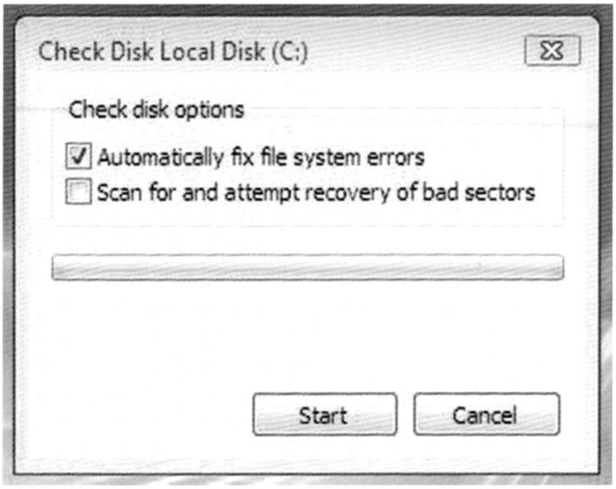

Fig.1.10 Two types of checking are available

program is easily accessed, and the first step is to go into Windows Explorer. Locate the entry for the drive you wish to check, right-click its entry, and then choose Properties from the pop-up menu. This produces a window like the one of Figure 1.8, which gives some basic information about the drive.

Operate the Tools tab to switch to a Window like the one in Figure 1.9, which includes an error checking facility. Left-clicking the Check Now button produces the small window of Figure 1.10, where two options are available via the checkboxes. The upper checkbox is ticked if you wish to check the filing system, but this check cannot be made while Windows is running. Using this option schedules the check to run the next time the computer is booted into Windows.

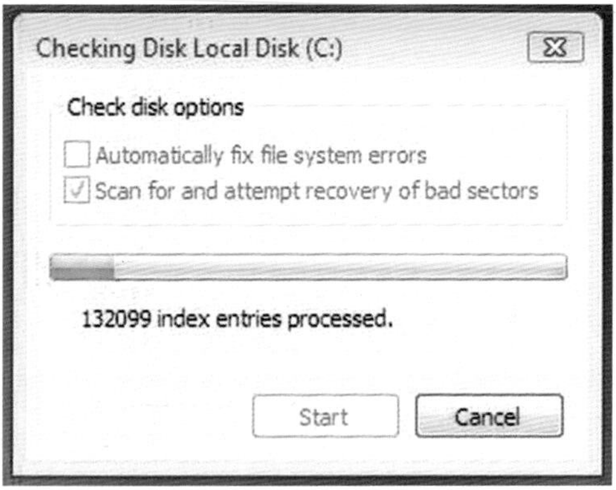

Fig.1.11 A bargraph shows how things are progressing

Using the facilities offered by the lower checkbox is more straightforward. This checks the disc for bad sectors, and using this option results in the disc being checked immediately. A bargraph at the bottom of the window shows how far the checking has progressed (Figure 1.11). Details of any bad sectors that have been found and removed will be provided when the scanning process has been completed. Of course, the program

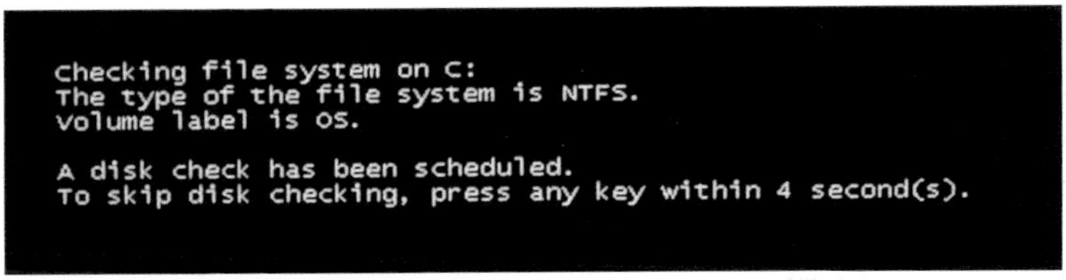

```
Checking file system on C:
The type of the file system is NTFS.
Volume label is OS.

A disk check has been scheduled.
To skip disk checking, press any key within 4 second(s).
```

Fig.1.12 The computer has rebooted and the checking has begun

does not actually remove the bad sectors. It simply maps them as unusable in the disc filing system so that the computer makes no further attempts to use them.

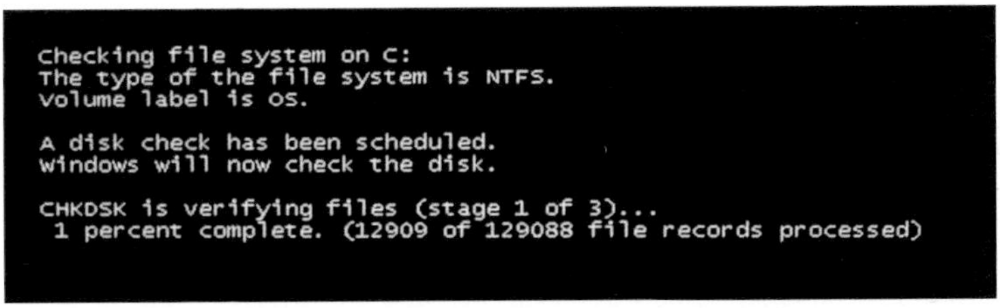

```
Checking file system on C:
The type of the file system is NTFS.
Volume label is OS.

A disk check has been scheduled.
Windows will now check the disk.

CHKDSK is verifying files (stage 1 of 3)...
  1 percent complete. (12909 of 129088 file records processed)
```

Fig.1.13 The checker program gives details of its progress

If you opt to have the file system checked, on starting the scan you will instead get a pop-up message that explains the need to provide the

```
Security descriptor verification completed.
  17367 data files processed.
CHKDSK is verifying Usn Journal...
100 percent complete. (36569088 of 36575736 USN bytes processed)
  36575736 USN bytes processed.
Usn Journal verification completed.
Windows has checked the file system and found no problems.

  477850623 KB total disk space.
   40544700 KB in 111240 files.
      65288 KB in 17368 indexes.
          0 KB in bad sectors.
     253183 KB in use by the system.
      65536 KB occupied by the log file.
  436987452 KB available on disk.

       4096 bytes in each allocation unit.
  119462655 total allocation units on disk.
  109246863 allocation units available on disk.

Windows has finished checking your disk.
Please wait while your computer restarts.
```

Fig.1.14 The check has been completed and there were no disc errors

scan before the computer boots into Windows. Opt to go ahead anyway, and then you are then asked if you would like to schedule the scan to be run automatically on the next occasion that the computer is booted into Windows. To go ahead with the checking and fixing process, operate the Yes button and restart the computer. The checking program will be launched during the boot process (Figure 1.12), before the boot drive is left with any open files. The screen will show how things are progressing (Figure 1.13), and the boot process will continue once the disc checker has completed its task (Figure 1.14). The disc file system used by Windows XP and Vista is less prone to problems than the systems used in early versions of Windows, and these operating systems are also better at sorting out problems before they have a chance to escalate. In most cases, as in this example, no problems will be detected.

Deletion

A program such as Disk Cleanup can remove certain types of file that are no longer required, but it cannot manage your data files for you. Only you know which data files are likely to be needed in the future and should be retained on the hard disc drive. The rest can be copied onto some form of removable media before they are deleted from the disc. Of course, it is not essential to make archive copies if you are sure that the files will never be needed again, but it is advisable to take copies "just in case".

You could try erasing programs and other files that are no longer needed, but this type of thing has to be undertaken with great care. In the days of MS/DOS it was perfectly acceptable to delete a program and any files associated with it if you no longer wished to use the program. Matters are very different with Windows, where most software is installed into the operating system. There are actually some simple programs that have just one file, and which do not require any installation. These standalone program files are quite rare these days, but they can be used much like old MS/DOS programs. To use the program you copy it onto the hard disc, and to run it you use the Run option from the Start menu, or locate the file using Windows Explorer and double-click on it. No installation program is used, and it is perfectly all right to remove the program by deleting the program file.

Most programs are installed onto the computer using an installation program, and this program does not simply make folders on the hard disc and copy files into them from the CD-ROM. It will also make changes to the Windows configuration files so that the program is properly integrated with the operating system. If you simply delete the program's directory structure to get rid of it, Windows will not be aware that the program has been removed. During the boot-up process the operating system will probably look for files associated with the deleted program, and will produce error messages when it fails to find them.

Matters are actually more involved than this, and there is another potential problem in that

Fig.1.15 There is an uninstaller for the AVG program

Windows utilizes shared files. This is where one file, such as a DLL type, is shared by two or more programs. In deleting a program and the other files in its directory structure you could also be deleting files needed by other programs. This could prevent other programs from working properly, or even from starting up at all.

If a program is loaded onto the hard disc using an installation program, the only safe way of removing it is to use an uninstaller program. There are three possible ways of handling this:

- **Custom uninstaller**
- **Windows built-in uninstaller**
- **Third-party uninstaller**

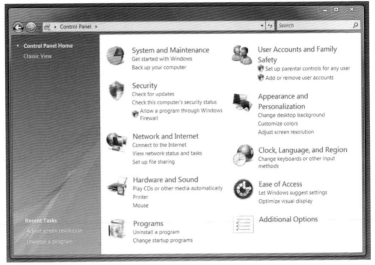

Fig.1.16 The normal version of the Windows Control Panel

Custom uninstaller

Some programs load an uninstaller program onto the hard disc as part of the installation process. This program is then available via the Start menu if you choose All Programs, and then the folder with the name of the program concerned. If there is no folder icon for the program, just the normal entry that is used to launch it, then that program does not have an uninstaller or other additional software available. Even if there is a folder icon for the program, it is possible that there will be no uninstall option available there. The example of Figure 1.15 shows the submenu for the AVG Antivirus program, and this one does include an option to uninstall the program. Uninstaller programs are almost invariably automatic in operation, so you have to do little more than instruct a program of this type to go ahead with the removal of the program.

With any uninstaller software you may be asked if certain files should be removed. This mostly occurs where the program finds shared files that no longer appear to be shared. In days gone by it did not seem to matter whether you opted to remove or leave these files. Either way, Windows usually failed to work properly thereafter! Things seem to be more reliable these days, and it is reasonably safe to accept either option.

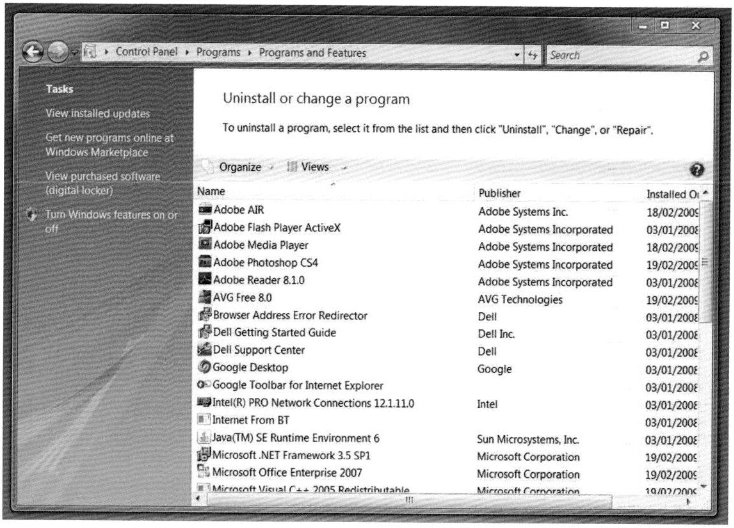

Fig.1.17 This window lists all the installed programs

To leave the files in place is certainly the safest option, but it also results in files and possibly folders being left on the disc unnecessarily.

Windows uninstaller

Windows has a built-in uninstaller that can be accessed via the control panel. From the Start menu select Control Panel, and in the Control Panel (Figure 1.16) left-click the Uninstall a Program link in the Programs section. This takes you to the uninstaller section of the Control Panel, and the main section of the screen shows a list of the programs that can be uninstalled via this route (Figure 1.17). Removing a program is basically just a matter of selecting it from the list by left-clicking its entry, and then operating the Uninstall/Change button.

The next step depends on the particular software that you are removing, and it may simply be necessary to confirm that you wish to remove the selected program. In many cases, and particularly in the case of major pieces of software, there will be more than one course of action open to you. In the example of Figure 1.18 there is a choice of installing or reinstalling the software, or removing it. In the current context, it is clearly the option of removing the program that is selected. The other option is

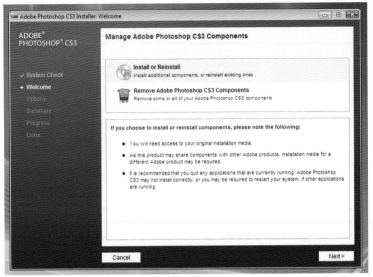

Fig.1.18 The program can be installed, reinstalled, or removed. Individual parts of the program or all of them can be removed

used when it is necessary to install optional extras that were not chosen when the software was originally installed, or where a program has become corrupted and is not functioning correctly.

Spanner in the works

If a PC gradually slows down over a long period of time it is likely that it is caused by the dreaded "software bloat". The situation is different when a PC suddenly slows down for no apparent reason. If some new software has been added, it could simply be that this is using the PC's resources and is slowing things down. Bear in mind that many programs insist on loading clever little utilities during the boot process. This obviously extends the boot process as there is more to load. Although the utilities simply run in the background doing very little most of the time, they still use up the computer's resources such as memory and processing time.

If no new software has been added, it is possible that the Windows installation has been damaged. The usual Windows troubleshooting techniques can be used in an attempt to cure the problem, the System Restore facility can be used to take the system back to a setup where it functioned properly. Another possible cause of the slow-down is that the computer has been infected with some form of computer pest.

This is a very real possibility if the PC is used on the Internet. It is important to realise that things have moved on from what might be termed the traditional computer virus. An ordinary virus attaches itself to other files and tries to propagate itself across the system and on to other systems if the opportunity arises. At some stage the virus will make its presence obvious by placing a message on the screen and (or) starting to damage files. Not all viruses try to do any real damage, but a substantial percentage of them will do so unless they are removed first.

A virus is unlikely to produce any noticeable reduction in speed with a modern PC, although this is something that cannot be totally discounted. However, there are other forms of pest that certainly will reduce some aspects of performance. This will often be in the form of a greatly extended boot-up period, and there can also be some general loss of speed thereafter. Disc accesses will often take longer than expected when a computer has been infected by a pest. The Internet connection running slowly is another possible symptom of a computer infection of some sort.

It is important to understand the differences between the various types of computer pest that are currently in circulation. Computer security has become more important with the rise in use of the Internet and Email. The original viruses were designed to spread themselves across any system whenever the opportunity arose. In most cases the purpose was to damage the file system of any infected computer. Many of the recent pests are more sinister than this, and in many cases will not actually try to cause significant damage to the file system. Instead, they aid hackers to hijack your PC, extract information from it such as passwords, or something of this nature. If a computer pest is causing your PC to run slowly this could be the least of your problems! The next sections briefly describe the various types of computer pest currently in circulation.

Virus

The non-technical press tend to call any form of software that attacks computers a virus, but it is a specific type of program. Initially, someone attaches the virus to a piece of software, and then finds a way of getting that software into computer systems. These days the Internet is the most likely route for the infection to be spread, but it is important not to overlook the fact that infections can also be spread via discs, Flash memory cards, and via a network. Once into a system a virus will attack that system and try to replicate itself. A virus spreads by attaching itself to other programs and files, which makes it more difficult to detect than an infection that exists as a separate program file. The infected files can sometimes be healed by removing the virus, but this is not always possible.

Script virus

These days you have to be suspicious of many types of file. Countless application programs such as word processors and spreadsheets now have the ability to automate tasks using scripts or macros as they are also known. The application effectively has a built-in programming language and the script or macro is a form of program. This makes it possible for viruses or other harmful programs to be present in many types of data file. Scripts are also used in some web pages, and viruses can be hidden in these as JavaScript programs, Java applets, etc. There are other potential sources of infection such as Email attachments.

Worm

A worm is a program that replicates itself, usually from one disc to another, or from one system to another via a local network or the Internet. In recent times many of the worldwide virus scares have actually been caused by worms transmitted via Email, and not by what would normally be accepted as a virus. The usual ploy is for the worm to send a copy of itself to every address in the Email address book of the infected system. A worm spread in this way, even if it is not intrinsically harmful, can have serious consequences. There can be a sudden upsurge in the amount of Email traffic, possibly causing parts of the Email system to seriously slow down or even crash. Some worms compromise the security of the infected system, perhaps enabling it to be used by a hacker for sending spam for example. This can obviously cause a major reduction in the speed at which programs run.

Trojan horse

A Trojan horse, or just plain Trojan as it is now often called, is a program that is supposed to be one thing but is actually another. In the early days many Trojans were in the form of free software, and in particular, free antivirus programs. The users obtained nasty shocks when the programs were run, with their computer systems being attacked. Like viruses, some Trojans do nothing more than display stupid messages, but others attack the disc files, damage the boot sector of the hard disc, and so on.

Backdoor Trojan

A backdoor Trojan is the same as the standard variety in that it is supplied in the form of a program that is supposed to be one thing but is actually another. In some cases nothing appears to happen when you install the program. In other cases the program might actually install and run as expected. In both cases one or two small programs will have been installed on the computer and set to run when the computer is booted.

One ploy is to have programs that produce log files showing which programs you have run and Internet sites that you have visited. The log will usually include any key presses as well. The idea is for the log file to provide passwords to things such as your Email account, online bank account, and so on. Someone hacking into your computer system will usually look for the log files, and could obviously gain access to important information from these files.

Another ploy is to have a program that makes it easier for hackers to break into your computer system. A backdoor Trojan does not attack the infected computer in the same way as some viruses, and it does not try to spread the infection to other discs or computers. Potentially though, a backdoor Trojan is more serious than a virus, particularly if you use the computer for online banking, share dealing, etc. Your computer can be expected to run very slowly if the Trojan results in it being used as a robot to send spam or something of this nature.

Spyware

Spyware programs monitor system activity and send information to another computer by way of the Internet. There are really two types of spyware, and one tries to obtain passwords and send them to another computer. This takes things a step further than the backdoor Trojan programs mentioned earlier. A backdoor Trojan makes it easier for a hacker to obtain sensitive information from your PC, but it does not go as far as sending any information that is placed in the log files. Spyware is usually hidden in other software in Trojan fashion.

Adware

The second type of spyware is more correctly called adware. In common with spyware, it gathers information and sends it to another computer via the Internet. Adware is not designed to steal passwords or other security information from your PC. Its purpose is usually to gather information for marketing purposes, and this typically means gathering and sending details of the web sites you have visited. Some free programs are supported by banner advertising, and the adware is used to select advertisements that are likely to be of interest to you.

Programs that are supported by adware have not always made this fact clear during the installation process. Sometimes the use of adware was pointed out in the End User License Agreement, but probably few people bother to read the "fine print". These days the more respectable software companies that use this method of raising advertising revenues make it clear that the adware will be installed together with the main program. There is often the option of buying a "clean" copy of the program. Others try to con you into installing the adware by using the normal tricks.

Provided you know that it is being installed and are happy to have it on your PC, adware is not a major security risk. It is sending information about your surfing habits, but you have given permission for it to do so. If you feel that this is an invasion of privacy, then do not consent to it being installed. The situation is different if you are tricked into installing adware. Then it does clearly become an invasion of your privacy and you should remove any software of this type from your PC. Note that if you consent to adware being installed on your PC and then change your mind, removing it will probably result in the free software it supports being disabled or uninstalled. Spyware increases the loading on the computer's microprocessor and it uses system resources. Consequently, it is likely to slow down the computer to some extent, but it is unlikely to massively affect performance on a modern PC. Some adware seems to cause other programs or the operating system to crash.

Diallers

A dialler is a program that uses a modem and an ordinary dial-up connection to connect your PC to another computer system. Diallers probably have numerous legitimate applications, but they are mainly associated with various types of scam. An early one was a promise of free pornographic material that required a special program to be downloaded. This program was, of course, the dialler, which proceeded to call a high cost number in a country thousands of miles away. In due course the user received an astronomic telephone bill. With a modern variation the user goes onto the Internet in the usual way via their dial-up connections, and everything might appear to be perfectly normal. However, the dialler is connecting them to a different ISP that is probably thousands of miles away and is again costing a fortune in telephone charges.

The increasing use of broadband Internet connections has largely or totally removed the threat of dialler related problems for many. If there is no ordinary telephone modem in your PC, there is no way the dialler can connect your PC to the Internet or another computer system via a dial-up connection. There is a slight risk if your PC is equipped with a telephone modem for sending and receiving faxes. The risk is relatively small though, since you would presumably notice that the modem was being used for no apparent reason.

Hoax virus

A hoax virus might sound innocuous enough and just a bit of a joke, but it has the potential to spread across the world causing damage to computer systems. The hoax is usually received in the form of an Email from someone that has contacted you previously. They say that the Email they sent you previously was infected with a virus, and the Email then goes on to provide information on how to remove the virus. This usually entails searching for one or more files on your PC's hard disc drive and erasing them.

Of course, there was no virus in the initial Email. The person that sent the initial Email could be the hoaxer, or they might have been fooled by the hoax themselves. The hoax Email suggests that you contact everyone that you have emailed recently, telling them that their computer could be infected and giving them the instructions for the "cure". This is the main way in which a hoax virus is propagated. The files that you are instructed to remove could be of no real consequence, or they could be important system files. It is best not to fall for the hoax and find out which they are.

Likely candidates

Several types of computer pest have the ability to slow down a PC and (or) extend the boot-up time. One of my PCs recently suffered from the slow boot-up problem and it also seemed to be slow when any disc accesses were involved. A good starting point if you suspect that there could be an "intruder" present in your PC is to use the Control-Alt-Delete key combination to bring up the Task Manager. With Windows Vista this key combination does not immediately produce the program, but instead brings up a menu screen where you can opt to run Task Manager (Figure 1.19). However, if preferred you can jump straight to Task Manager by using the Control - Shift - Escape key combination, or by right-clicking the taskbar and then left-clicking Task Manager in the drop-down menu. Once Task Manager is running you can look for any programs or processes that should not be there. If you are not sure about any of them it is easy to find details using a search engine such as Google.

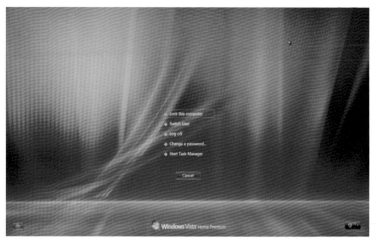

Fig.1.19 This screen has an option to run Task Manager

Use the name of the process plus the word "process" as the search string, and several links to sites giving basic details of the process should be obtained.

A program called Hijackthis is available as a free download from the usual sources such as download.com, and this can be used to show a list of changes to the system and suspicious processes. However, be aware that most of the things it lists will be perfectly legitimate processes and changes. In order to use a program such as this you need a fair amount of expertise, or must obtain specialist help from one of the sites that offer assistance in dealing with computer infections.

Having found a malicious program by whatever means, you can use the normal search facilities of Windows Explorer to locate and delete the offending program file. Do not be surprised if the offending program simply reappears the next time the computer is booted into Windows. Many modern computer pests are designed so that a file is installed and run each time the computer is booted into the operating system. Hence the deleted program runs again when the computer is rebooted.

Free protection

In order to permanently remove most modern computer infections it is necessary to use an antivirus program. New PCs are almost invariably supplied complete with a commercial antivirus program, but this usually

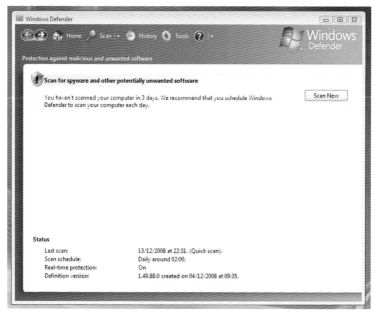

Fig.1.20 The Windows Defender information window

has a fairly short subscription to updates. After a month or three the virus database is no longer updated with details of new viruses, and the program then becomes less and less effective with the passage of time.

There are better ways of handling things than continuing to use a commercial antivirus program that is relying on out of date virus definitions. Windows Vista does actually have a built-in program that is designed to protect the computer from various types of threat, and it is called Windows Defender. This is normally included as part of a standard Windows Vista installation, so it will almost certainly run automatically each time your computer is switched on.

Windows Defender runs in the background, protecting your computer all the time it is switched on. The main program can be accessed by going to the Start menu, selecting All Programs, and then choosing Windows Defender from the menu. This produces a window like the one shown in Figure 1.20, which provides information about the last time that Windows Defender did a scan of the system. A scan can be started manually by operating the Scan Now button, and in due course this will

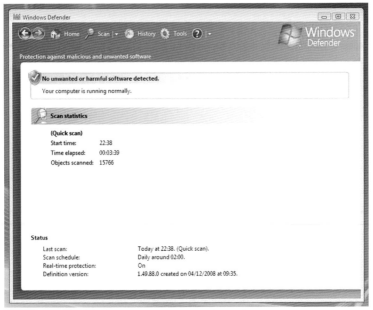

Fig.1.21 In this example no threats were found

provide the scan results. No threats were found in the example of Figure 1.21, and therefore none were removed from the system.

Fig.1.22 Operate the Options button

It is possible to control the way in which Windows Defender operates by first left-clicking the Tools icon near the top of the window, which changes it to look like Figure 1.22. Next operate the Options button, and the window will then change to the one shown in Figure 1.23. There are various parameters that can

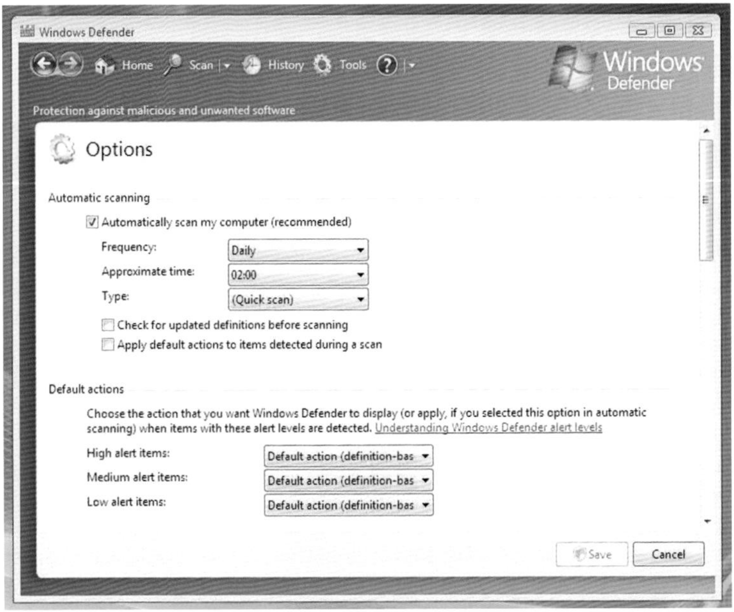

Fig.1.23 The time at which scanning takes places can be changed

be altered here, but in most cases the default settings will suffice. However, you might like to alter the time at which automatic scanning takes place. The default is usually for this to occur at about 2:00 in the morning, when it is unlikely that your computer will be running. A more suitable time can then be selected from the pop-down menu.

As with most software of this general type, the program can undertake a quick scan or a more thorough type. Obviously a thorough scan is preferable, but each scan of this type can take a very long time. In fact with many PCs it takes too long to be practical for daily scanning. Quick scanning is then the more practical choice, perhaps with the occasional full scan started manually. Of course, it is not necessary to have a daily scan at all, and one of the menus offers scans at other intervals. The scanning can be switched off completely by removing the tick in the "Automatically scan my computer" checkbox.

Other programs

Windows Defender is primarily designed to counter spyware and pop-up advertisements on web pages, and it is not intended to be a complete solution to problems with malicious software. It should be used in addition to antivirus software rather than instead of it. If you do not wish to pay for a subscription to commercial antivirus software there are some good free alternatives available.

One option is to use a free online virus checking facility to periodically scan your PC, but the drawback of this method is that there is no real-time protection for your PC. By the time you do a virus scan it is possible that a virus could have been spreading across your files for some time. By the time it is detected and removed it is likely that a significant amount of damage would already have been done.

An antivirus program running on your PC will, like Windows Defender, provide real-time protection. In other words, it monitors disc drive activity, Internet activity, or anything that might involve a virus or other malicious program. If any suspicious files are detected, there is an attempt to alter system files, or any dubious activity is detected, the user is warned. In most cases the virus or other malicious program is blocked or removed from the system before it has a chance to do any harm.

The alternative to using online virus scanning is to download and install a free antivirus program. There are one or two totally free antivirus programs available on the Internet, where you do not even have to pay for any online updates to the database. The free version of AVG 8.0 from Grisoft is one that is certainly worth trying. The Grisoft site is at:

www.grisoft.com

On the home page there might be a link to the free version of the program, but it does not seem to feature quite as prominently in the home page as it did in the past. At the time of writing this, the web address for Grisoft's free software is:

http://free.avg.com/download-avg-anti-virus-free-edition

There is an instruction manual for the program in PDF format, and it is possible to read this online provided your PC has the Adobe Acrobat Reader program installed. However, it is definitely a good idea to download the manual and store it on the hard disc drive so that it is handy for future reference. It is a good idea to at least take a quick look through the manual which, amongst other things, provides installation instructions. However, installation is fairly straightforward and follows along the normal lines for Windows software.

Fig.1.24 The main window of the AVG Free program

Daily updates to AVG are available free of charge, so although free, it should always be reasonably up-to-date. This program has a reputation for being very efficient, and it did once detect a couple of backdoor Trojan programs on my system that a certain well known commercial program had failed to detect. It is certainly one of the best freebies on the Internet, and it generally performs very well in comparison to commercial equivalents.

AVG has a useful range of facilities and it is a very capable program. Like Windows Defender, it runs in the background and provides real-time protection, but you can also go into the main program. It can be launched via the normal routes, and by default there will be a quick-launch button near the bottom left-hand corner of the Windows Desktop. The program has various sections, and the initial window provides access to them (Figure 1.24). There is a facility here that manually updates the program's virus database, but the program will automatically update provided an active Internet link is available when the program is booted into Windows. In common with most antivirus programs you can set it to scan the system on a regular basis.

Fig.1.25 The main Windows Update window

It is only fair to point out that an antivirus program cannot automatically remove every type of computer infection. Most can be dealt with automatically, but some have to be removed manually. In such cases the program will usually provide removal instructions, or take you to a web site where detailed instructions can be found. Some of the steps required can be a bit technical, but everything should be fine provided you follow the instructions "to the letter". However, if you have a friend or relative who has a fair amount of computing expertise, enlisting their help is probably a good idea, for peace of mind if nothing else.

Automatic updates

Last, and by no means least, keep your software, especially the operating system and file browsers, fully up-to-date, Hackers try to exploit weaknesses in Windows, browsers and other software that make the programs vulnerable to attack. The software writers are continually finding ways of making their programs more resilient against attacks, and soon find ways of fixing any flaws in their programs. This results in frequent updates being made available for Windows, and slightly less frequently for many other programs. Some updates are not security related, and

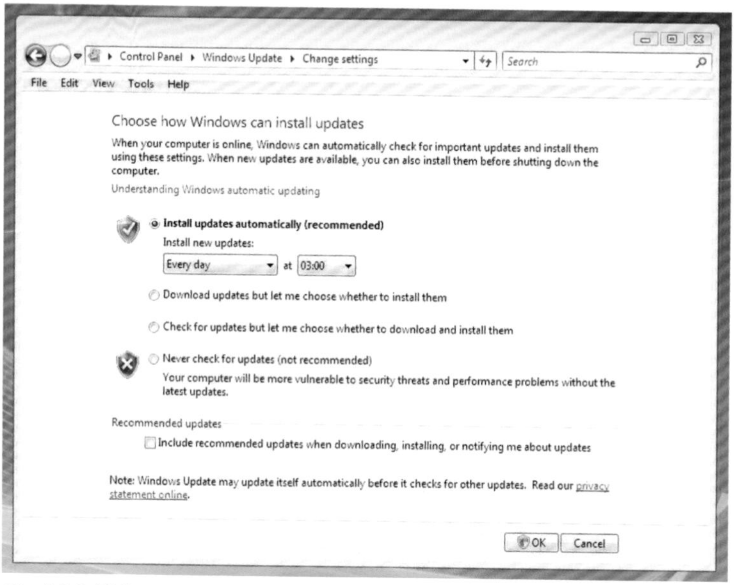

Fig.1.26 This window is used to schedule automatic updating

installing them is not crucial. This is not to say that they are not worthwhile, as the changes to the program will usually fix minor problems, add new features, or improve existing ones. However, failing to install them will not leave your computer at risk.

The same is not true of security updates, and it is important to have these installed at the earliest possible opportunity. Without them your computer is left at risk of attack, and it will be especially vulnerable if you use some form of broadband Internet connection. Keeping Windows up-to-date and installing any security updates is especially important. Without them it is possible that hackers could take over your PC, steal sensitive information stored on it, or use it for illegal attacks on other computers. For the same reason it is also important to keep your web browser up-to-date.

Windows Vista has a built-in update facility that is accessed by going to the Classic version of the Control Panel and double-clicking the Windows Update icon. This launches the window shown in Figure 1.25, and the upper section of the main panel provides details of any updates that are available. The control button gives the option of actually installing them, should you wish to do so.

An alternative way of tackling Windows updates is to opt for them to be installed automatically. This method of updating might have been set up when Windows was installed, but if not it can be selected by operating the Change Settings link in the left-hand section of the Control Panel. It then changes to look like Figure 1.26, where there are various update options available. The simplest approach is to have all updates installed automatically, and this is a good way of doing things if the computer is normally connected to a fast broadband connection. This method is probably not a practical proposition if a slower Internet connection is used, such as a dial-up type, or it is only used occasionally with a fast connection.

A more selective approach is then a better way of going about things, as it is then possible to opt out of any large downloads that will be of little or no benefit to you. The option to select is the one that lets you choose the updates and then downloads only those that have been selected. The other option downloads all updates and then lets you choose the ones you wish to actually install. This method does not reduce the amount of update data that is downloaded, but could still have the slight advantage of preventing hard disc space being consumed by unnecessary updates.

Processes

Background processes are important to modern computing and provide a number of useful tasks. For example, an antivirus program running in the background can protect your PC from infection, dealing with viruses and computer pests before they have a chance to do any harm. The problem with background processes is that too many of them running at once can hog a PC's resources. The processing time and memory used by each process will probably be quite small, but with say ten processes running, the overall drain on the PC's resources could be considerable. In fact having a large number of these processes running simultaneously would almost certainly slow down even the most potent of PCs.

A big problem with background processes is that many of them are installed automatically when applications programs are loaded onto a PC. The installation program might explain that a background process will be installed, and there is sometimes an option to omit it from the installation. In practice few users pay any attention to these options when installing new software. If you simply opt for "default" or "typical" installations it is likely that your PC will soon be running some additional background tasks.

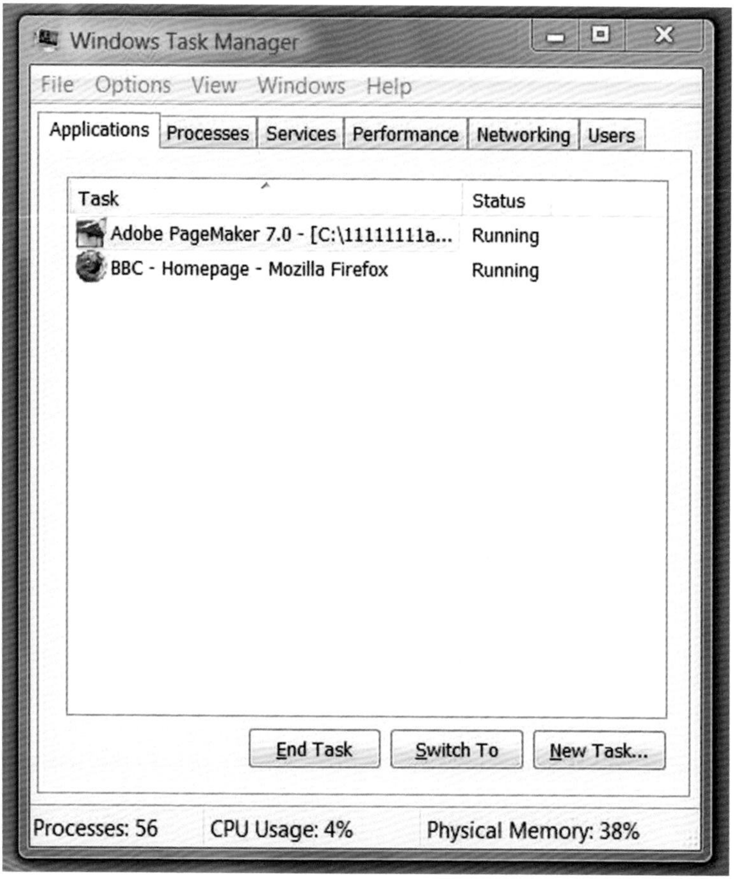

Fig.1.27 The Applications section of Windows Task Manager

The exact purpose of many background processes is something less than obvious, but many of them are intended to make things happen faster when using a certain facility of an application program. This is fine if you make frequent use of the program and facility in question, but the overhead on the PC's performance is unlikely to be justified in the case of an infrequently used feature. Where possible, it makes sense to suppress background tasks that do not "earn their keep".

As explained previously, the Windows Task Manager program can be used to show the processes that are running on a PC. Using Windows

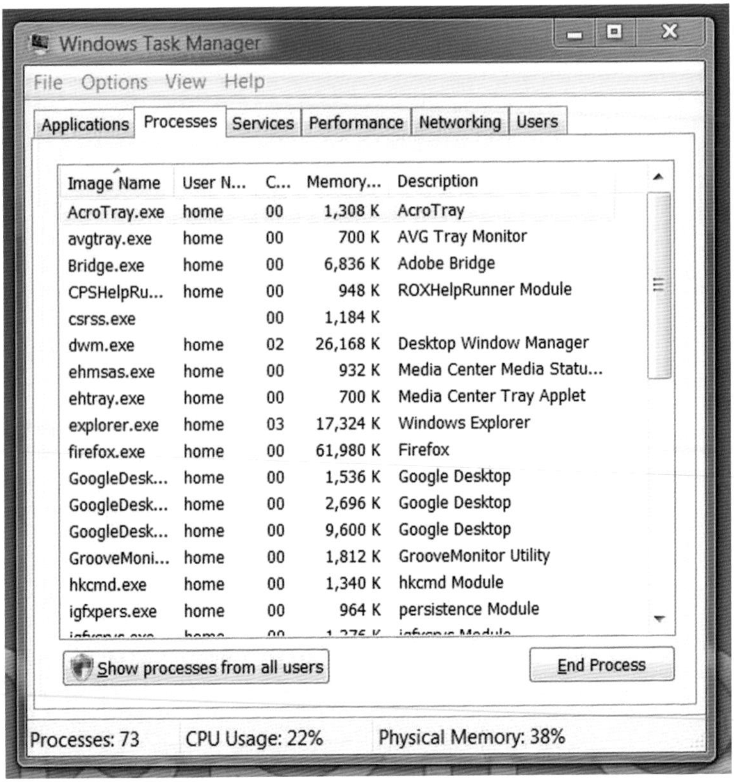

Fig.1.28 In this case it is the Processes section that is of interest

Vista it is either a matter of using the traditional Control-Alt-Delete key combination, and then selecting Start Task Manager from the menu screen that appears (refer back to Figure 1.19), or jumping straight to it using the Control-Shift-Escape key combination, or as described on page 25.   Either way, you will end up with Task Manager running in a small window on the Vista Desktop. In the current context it is only the entries under the Processes tab that are of interest (Figure 1.27).

Task Manager lists applications programs and processes separately, and by default it will probably list any applications programs you are running at the time. Operate the Processes tab to produce a list of the background processes that are running (Figure 1.28). The list will be pretty long, but a substantial proportion of the processes will be part of Windows. For example, all the entries marked "SYSTEM" in the User Name column are part of the operating system. The ones that have the name of the current user in this column are the background tasks that are probably optional.

The process program files often have cryptic names, but in most cases the Description field names the program that is associated with each process. Another way to identify processes is to use the name of the process in an Internet search engine such as Google, together with something like "Task Manager" or "background processes". There are a number of sites that give details of all the background processes that they have managed to identify, and the search will probably lead you to one of these.

On looking down the list of processes associated with application programs you will probably find a few programs that you do not use. This can be due to programs that you once used regularly having fallen from favour, or there could be preinstalled software that was supplied with the computer but is never used. In either case, uninstalling the software will free some hard disc space and prevent the program from using the computers resources by running background tasks.

There could be some background tasks that can be switched off even in cases where you do still use the main program. The Preferences dialogue box for the program might give the option of switching off a quick-launch facility for example. Uninstallers sometimes give the option of changing the program's setup in addition to simply uninstalling it. Failing that, it should be possible to uninstall the program and then reinstall it again with the unwanted features omitted. Ideally you should endeavour to opt out of optional features that are not needed when software is initially installed, thus avoiding the need to find a way of removing it later.

Note that you cannot get rid of a process by selecting it in Task Manager and operating the End Process button. This method will in fact switch off most processes, but it is a rather clumsy way of handling things since it would be necessary to use this method each time the PC was booted. Any unnecessary processes should be prevented from automatically starting at switch-on, and not by switching them off once they have started running.

Sidebar

The Windows Sidebar is a new feature that was introduced with Windows Vista, and it is probably a useful feature that is used by millions of people.

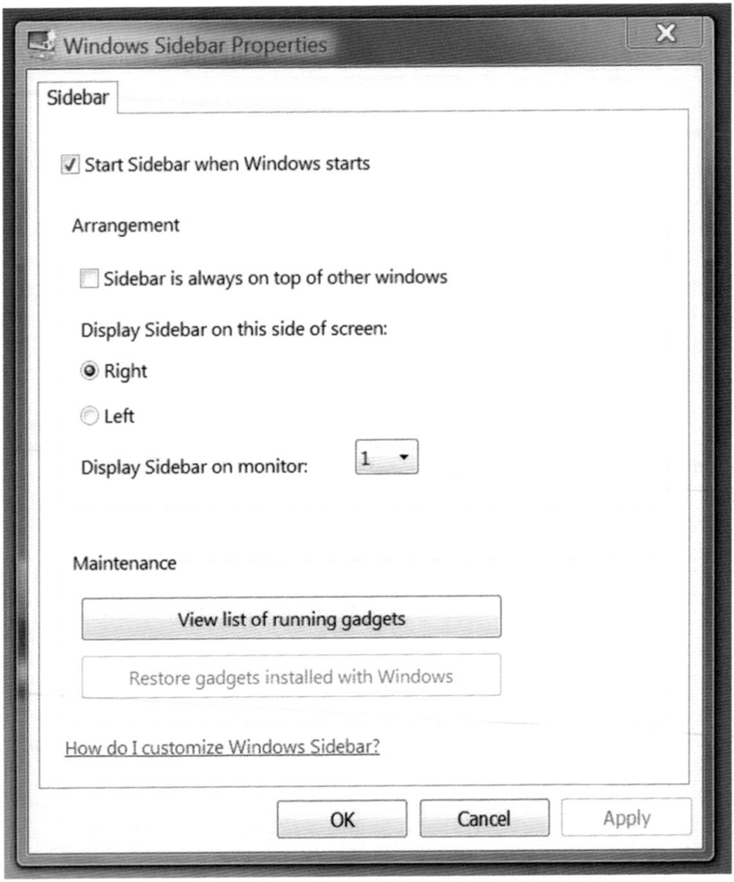

Fig.1.29 The Sidebar Properties window

On the other hand, if you are not one of those millions it is just an annoyance and a waste of the computer's resources. It is not an essential part of Windows Vista, and there is no need to have the sidebar automatically started when the computer boots into Windows.

In order to prevent it from starting automatically, first right-click the Sidebar's icon in the Taskbar and then select Properties from the pop-up menu. The Taskbar is normally positioned along the bottom of the screen, and the icon for the Sidebar should be in the group of icons at the right end of the Taskbar. If there are more than about four icons in the group they will not all be displayed. Hidden icons can be shown by left-clicking the arrow at the left end of the group. When the Sidebar Properties window appears (Figure 1.29), remove the tick from the checkbox near the very top of the Window and then operate the OK button. This will not switch off the Sidebar immediately, but it will prevent it from being launched automatically on subsequent occasions when the computer is booted into Windows.

To make it launch automatically again it is just a matter of going back to the Sidebar Properties window and ticking the checkbox again. Note that the Sidebar is still available even if it is not launched automatically at start-up. It can be launched manually by double-clicking its icon on the Taskbar.

Slow Desktop icons

A common problem with most versions of Windows is that of the Desktop icons taking a long time to appear on the Desktop when you exit an application program and return to the Desktop screen. In some cases they do not display properly, and you get a simplified icon instead. This problem is usually caused by the memory cache for the icons being too small to accommodate them all. Presumably the excess icons are stored in virtual memory, or on the hard disc drive in other words.

I am not aware of any easy way of increasing the size of the cache for the desktop icons. I once found a free utility program on the Internet that would increase the cache size for computers running Windows XP, and possibly something similar is available for Windows Vista. Incidentally, never use Windows utilities unless they are designed for the particular version of Windows that you are using. Running a utility for a different version is unlikely to have the desired effect, and could easily result in damage to the operating system.

Of course, the easy solution to this problem is not to clutter the desktop with dozens of icons. The desktop provides a quick and easy dumping ground for all sorts of files and shortcuts, but it is not really meant to be used in this way. It provides an easy way of accessing programs or files that you will use very often, and it can also be useful for storing files that will be stored on a temporary basis. It is not really meant to provide a means of launching every piece of software on your computer, accessing numerous files, and as a general storage area.

The approved cure when the Windows Desktop starts to refresh very slowly is to reduce the number of icons until it starts to operate at a more acceptable rate. Does everything on the Desktop really need to be there,

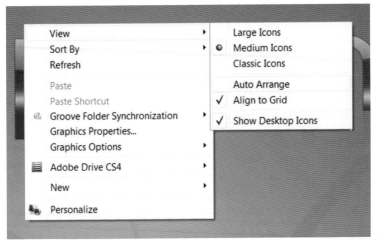

Fig.1.30 Remove the tick from the Auto Arrange option

or are there icons representing temporary files that are no longer needed, shortcuts to programs that you hardly ever use, and so on? Windows Vista and XP both have a pop-up utility that will warn you from time-to-time if there are unused icons on the desktop. Rather than simply closing this program, try using it to see if there are icons that you could usefully delete. If there are files on the Desktop that you still need, transfer them to a folder and make a shortcut to that folder. With this method you still have easy access to the files, but there is only one icon on the Desktop.

Stubborn icons

While on the subject of Desktop icons, a common complaint about them is their insistence on lining up in columns on the left-hand side of the screen. Each new icon positions itself at the bottom of the right-most column. Dragging an icon out of position and repositioning on the screen results in it immediately jumping back to its original place. There is an easy solution that enables icons to be positioned wherever you like on the screen, and that is to right-click a vacant area of the Desktop, select View from the pop-up menu (Figure 1.30), and then remove the tick from Auto Arrange in the submenu that appears. Also remove the tick from the Align to Grid option if you require complete freedom in the positioning of the icons, but the screen generally looks neater if the icons are aligned with an invisible onscreen grid.

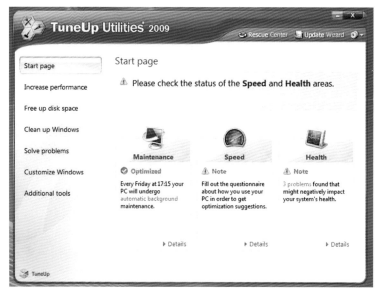

Fig.1.31 The initial screen of the TuneUp Utilities program

Tuning utilities

There are plenty of tuning utilities available for computers that use Windows, but you need to be careful when using any software of this type. Firstly, make sure that it is intended for use with the version of Windows that you are running. Using a tune-up utility designed for use with something other than the version of Windows you are actually using could result in the operating system being seriously damaged instead of streamlined. Also make sure that the program you are intending to use is from a reputable software company. Unfortunately, some unscrupulous companies have used software of this type as a means of installing various pieces of adware, etc., onto users' computers. Reading reviews of various programs on the Internet and in the computer press should help you to avoid programs that are not what they seem, or simply do not work very well.

Most tuning utilities work best if they are used regularly, starting when the computer is fairly new. In other words, they work well when used periodically to prevent a computer that is going well from starting to seriously slow down. A tune-up program, despite its name, is unlikely to

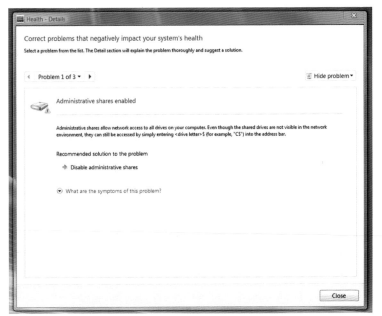

Fig.1.32 This section of the program gives recommendations about security issues

perform a few tweaks and restore a very sluggish PC back to full speed. A program of this type may provide a worthwhile improvement, but it will not perform miracles, even if the advertising literature suggests otherwise! It is better to keep PCs in fine fettle using some regular maintenance rather than letting them get seriously out of kilter and then trying to sort things out.

What does a tune-up program actually do? To some extent a program of this type simply performs tasks of the type described in previous sections of this book, and most of them at least partially duplicate the built-in system maintenance tools of Windows. However, most will provide additional features, such as a facility that checks the Windows Registry and tries to correct any errors that are found. Perhaps the main attraction of these programs is that most of them will perform a wide range of tasks automatically, or by running one program. This makes them very quick and convenient to use.

Fig.1.33 The Speed Optimiser utility has produced numerous suggestions

Another advantage of some tune-up programs is that they operate as a sort of expert system that analyses the system, makes recommendations, explains them, and if you agree, implements them for you. TuneUp Utilities is one of the better known and well established tuning utility suites, and the window of Figure 1.31 appears when it is first run. There are various options available here, including a questionnaire that helps the program to optimise the speed of your PC. Another section helps to identify and rectify security issues (Figure 1.32).

The program will come up with various recommendations if you use the Speed Optimiser facility (Figure 1.33). This helps to identify unnecessary background processes and stop them from running automatically at start-up, optimise the Internet settings to the operating environment of the computer, and so on. It can take some time to go through all the available options with a comprehensive tune-up program such as this, but it is very much easier and quicker than using the built-in utilities of Windows, and it is probably more thorough as well.

Fig.1.34 The crucial.com home page

Hardware upgrade

If you computer is set up efficiently but is still not working particularly quickly, it is time to face up to the fact that the hardware is inadequate to run Windows and your application programs any faster. Either a newer and faster PC is required, or the old PC must be given a hardware upgrade. Most hardware upgrades go beyond the scope of this book, and many do not really justify the time, effort, and money involved. There are two types that are relatively simple and are often cost-effective. These are to fit a better video card and to increase the amount of memory.

Video card upgrades will not be considered in detail here because a better video card actually makes very little difference with most types of computing. In fact the video card used makes no significant difference with application software that has a text or 2D graphics display. It is really with games and other applications that use clever 3D graphics displays that an up-market video card provides real benefits. It can be an expensive upgrade though. Using a lower screen resolution and (or)

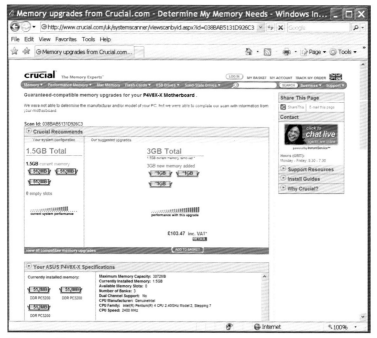

Fig.1.35 The scan results detail the existing memory and also include advice on upgrading

reduced colour depth provides a free means of obtaining a smoother 3D graphics display, and probably offers a better solution for many people.

On the face of it, fitting additional memory will not make a PC run any faster. The processor will still run at the same speed, so surely the PC will run no faster than it did prior to the memory upgrade? When running simple applications software this is probably true, and any increase in speed is unlikely. However, with the more demanding applications or when running several programs at once, increasing the amount of memory can give a significant increase in speed. When a PC has large amounts of memory, most of this memory is used as temporary storage space for data. If a PC has only a small amount of memory, it is soon used up and the hard disc is then used for storing temporary data. The disc is far slower than memory, and this is reflected in the speed at which heavyweight programs run on a PC that has limited memory capacity.

Of course, adding some extra memory is unlikely to bring much benefit if your PC already has a few gigabytes installed. In fact it might not be

Fig.1.36 The notch in the bottom of this memory module prevents it
from being fitted the wrong way around

possible to add more memory to a computer that is already fitted with a substantial amount. Bear in mind that the normal (32-bit) versions of Windows can only use a maximum of 3 or 3.5 gigabytes. A 64-bit version of Windows must be used in order to use more than that.

The most difficult task when undertaking a memory upgrade is to determine the exact type and size of memory module required. In some cases it is possible to retain the existing memory in the computer, and just add one or two more memory modules. This is not always a practical proposition though, and it is clearly out of the question if there are no vacant slots for additional modules. Practical experience suggests that it is better to abandon the existing memory and start from scratch. This way you can be sure that the memory modules are of precisely the same type and specification.

Using memory modules that have slightly different specifications is generally accepted as likely to cause problems, and using memory modules of different capacities is definitely not recommended. Modern main boards do not usually require memory modules to be used in pairs, which is something that was often a requirement in the past, but it might be necessary to use pairs of modules in order to obtain the best performance.

Some online assistance is very helpful for those with plenty of experience at memory upgrades, and it is virtually essential for beginners. The Crucial web site (www.crucial.com/uk) is one of the most helpful, and there is a Scan button on the home page (Figure 1.34). Strictly speaking this does not produce an online scan, because it takes you to a page where a program file can be downloaded, but no installation is needed with this file. It is simply downloaded to your Desktop, and double-clicking its icon then runs the memory scan.

The scan results (Figure 1.35) show the memory currently fitted to the computer, and gives details of the type or types of memory module that can be used. If it is essential to use pairs of modules, or if it is necessary to do so in order to obtain optimum performance, this information will be

Fig.1.37 This memory module has not been locked in place

included. Where a memory upgrade is possible, details of some possible upgrades are provided. The Crucial home page has an alternative to the memory scanning program, and this is to choose a few menu options that identify your PC. Advice on memory upgrades is then provided, but the recommendations do not take the existing memory into account. Of course, this is not important if you intend to scap the existing memory and start from scratch.

Fitting memories

Memory modules were produced in an attempt to make fitting and removing memory much easier than the old method of plugging numerous memory chips into holders. Fitting DIMMs (dual in-line memory modules) is certainly very easy, and it is impossible to fit them the wrong way round because the circuit board has a polarising "key". This is just an off-centre notch cut in the circuit board (Figure 1.36) that matches a bar in the DIMM socket. In fact there are often two of these keys, and they are apparently in slightly different positions depending on the supply voltage of the module and the type of RAM fitted. This should make it impossible to fit a DIMM of the wrong type.

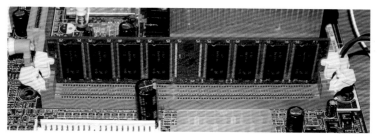

Fig.1.38 Here the module is fully in position and locked in place

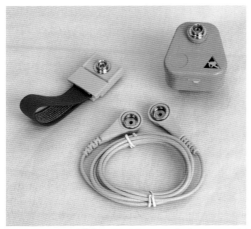

Fig.1.39 An anti-static wristband helps to avoid expensive damage

When fitting a DIMM always look for the notch that is well off centre. This, plus the bar in the socket, makes it clear which way round the module must be fitted. The module simply drops into place vertically and as it is pressed down into position the plastic lever at each end of the socket should start to close up. Pressing both levers into the vertical position should securely lock the module in place. Of course, the two levers must be set fully downwards and outwards before you start to insert the module.

Do not try to fit these modules by simply pressing hard until they click into place. They will probably fit into place correctly using this method, but it risks damaging the motherboard. Operating the levers enables modules to be fully inserted into their sockets without having to exert much force on the modules and motherboard. Figures 1.37 and 1.38 respectively show a DIMM before and after it has been locked into place. To remove a DIMM, simply press the two levers outwards as far as they will go. This should unlock the memory module so that it can be lifted free of the socket.

It is important to remember that most computer components are easily damaged by static charges, and that in this respect memory modules are one of the most vulnerable components. The safe way to handle memory modules, or any other static-sensitive components, is to earth yourself via one of the special wristbands (Figure 1.39) that are available from computer and electronic component suppliers. These earth the user to the mains earth connection via a couple of high value resistors that ensure good safety. Any static charge in the user's body is leaked away to earth before it has a chance to build up to a significant voltage. When using one of these wristbands you can therefore handle sensitive semiconductor components without any significant risk of accidentally zapping them.

Windows and
general fixes

Shutdown problems

At one time it was very common for computers running Windows to have problems with the system stalling during the shutting down process. In fact shutting down problems were far more common than starting up difficulties, but of less consequence. If a computer stalls during the shutting down process, the simple expedients of switching off the power or unplugging it from the mains supply will bring things to a halt, and the computer will almost certainly start up properly when it is switched on again. Do not switch off the power if the computer is providing an onscreen message to the effect that updates are being installed. Automatic updates to Windows are normally installed at the end of a computing session, prior to Windows closing and switching off the computer. Switching off the power while updates are being installed could damage the operating system and cause problems when the computer is next booted into Windows.

The usual cause of shutting down problems is a piece of software that will not stop working, resulting in Windows waiting indefinitely for it to close so that it can in turn close down. Sometimes the computer will actually close down if you wait long enough, but in many cases it will just hang indefinitely. You can try using the Control-Alt-Delete keyboard combination to run Task Manager, but this will only work if Windows is still largely operational. Finding and switching off the offending program using Task Manager might be ineffective anyway.

Windows Vista and XP are less prone to this problem than earlier versions of Windows because they will usually detect the rogue software and terminate it prior to shutting down the system. The operating system usually provides an onscreen message stating that a certain program or process is still running, and that it will terminate the offending software in a certain number of seconds. In most cases the software will be switched

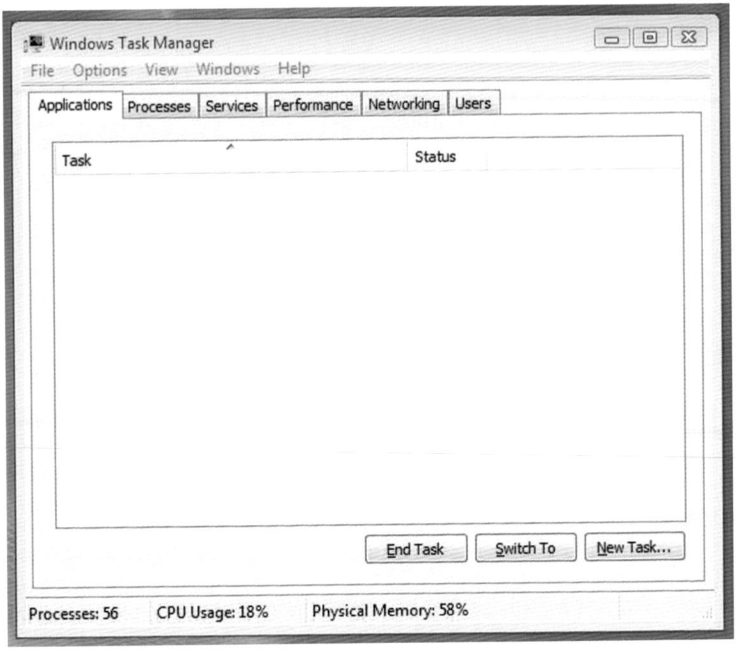

Fig.2.1 Task Manager is not listing any programs that are running

off successfully, and the operating system then shuts down normally. In a way it is irrelevant whether the computer eventually shuts down or it hangs-up. Either way there is a problem if it keeps happening.

Strictly speaking, this is not a problem with Windows itself, but is instead a problem with a program of some kind. It can be due to a faulty driver program for a piece of hardware, although in my experience this is not usually the cause. Problems with defective driver software usually surface long before you shut down the computer! It is more likely to be caused by an application program, or a piece of utility software such as an antivirus program. It can also be caused by a malicious program such as a Trojan or a virus.

The usual approach to identifying the offending software is to run Task Manager (Control-Shift-Escape or as described on page 25) prior to shutting down the computer, and having first checked that all application programs have been shut down. Unfortunately, in most cases it is not as simple as looking to see if an application is still running. Operating the Applications tab of Windows Task Manager will almost certainly show

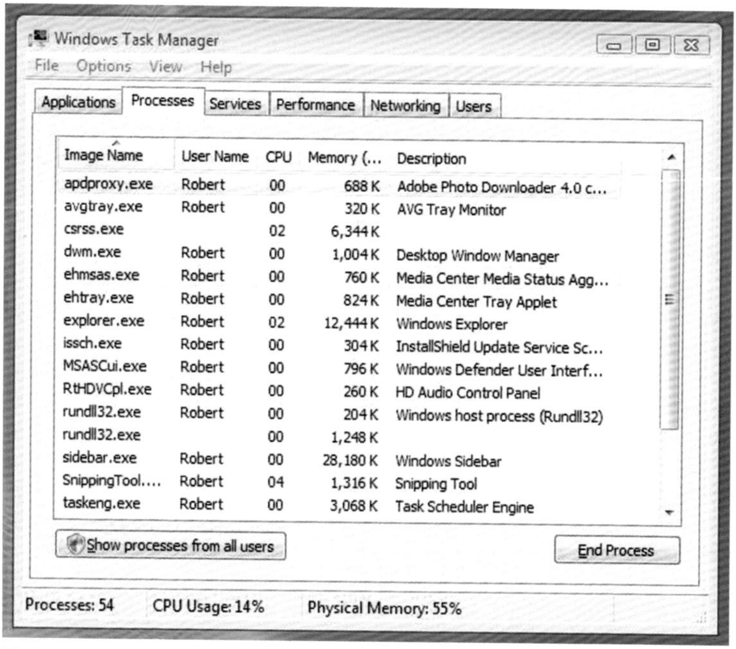

Fig.2.2 There are no programs running, but plenty of running processes are listed in Task Manager

that there are no programs running (Figure 2.1). If there is an entry here, then you are lucky and have identified the rogue program straight away. The window for the application has closed, but it is still running in the background.

It is more likely that no application has been left running, and that the problem is due to a process of some kind that is associated with an application program. The program should terminate the process before switching itself off, but for some reason it is failing to do so. Operating the Processes tab of Task Manager will produce a long list of processes that are running in the background (Figure 2.2), and many of these are associated with the operating system and will have "System" in the User field. Others are associated with application software and will have the name of the user currently logged onto the system. These processes are often something like a quick-launch utility that enables the application to start running more quickly than if it is started from scratch, or part of an antivirus program.

The obvious problem here is that many of these processes are not running in error, even though the application software that they are linked to is not operational. This makes it difficult to find a process that is still running when it should have been terminated earlier. It is often a matter of using trial and error to find the rogue process.   Work your way through the likely processes, terminating one of them using Task Manager each time the computer is shut down. In order to terminate a program it is just a matter of left-clicking its entry to select it, and then operating the End Process button.

If you end a process and the computer then shuts down correctly, it is virtually certain that you have located the source of the problem.   The Description field should give the name of the main program associated with that particular process, so always make a mental note of this before terminating a process and shutting down the computer. Having located the rogue program, uninstalling and then reinstalling it again will often provide a cure. If that does not work, the Support section of the program manufacturer's web site might have details of a fix, or installing the latest update might solve the problem.   Otherwise it is a matter of contacting the Customer Support service to see if they can help.

Registry problem?

It has been assumed so far that any shutting down problems are due to a piece of rogue software rather than an innate problem in Windows itself. A piece of software that does not terminate correctly is by far the most common reason for this problem, but in rare cases it can be caused by a hitch in Windows itself. One possible source of this problem is an error in the Windows Registry. In fact a Registry error is behind many Windows problems where the system behaves in an odd or erratic fashion.

The Windows Registry is a database that contains various operating parameters for Windows itself, and for any substantial piece of application software. When you change things like the screen resolution, the background for the Windows Desktop, or practically any aspect of Windows, you are actually changing one or more entries in the Registry. Those who know what they are doing can alter parameters by directly editing the Registry rather than by using the built-in facilities of Windows. Directly tweaking the Registry used to be a common practice among Windows experts as it permitted some changes that could not be achieved by other means. It now seems to be far less popular than in the past. Anyway, it is certainly something **that should not be attempted by those**

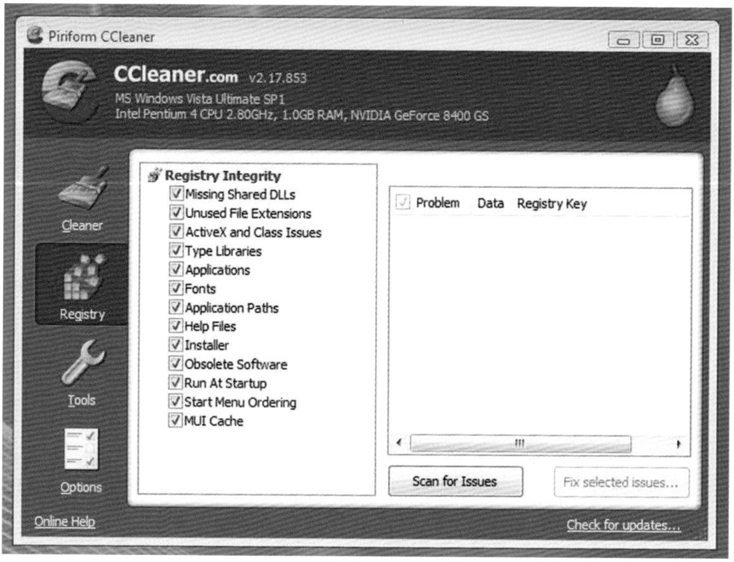

Fig.2.3 Ccleaner lists aspects of the Registry that can be checked

who lack the necessary expertise. When directly altering the Registry it is easy to get it slightly wrong and make matters worse instead of curing the problem.

The normal approach to curing Windows Registry problems is to use a utility program that searches the Registry for errors, and fixes any that it finds. No program of this type can be guaranteed to work perfectly every time, and the program should enable a backup copy of the Registry to be made before it undertakes the scanning and correction process. It is then possible to revert to the backup copy if the Registry fixing program should happen to make things worse rather than better. However, it is definitely better not to get into this situation in the first place, and it is important to use a Registry checker that is tried, tested, and as reliable as it could reasonably be.

The program used in this example is Ccleaner, which is free, but you can make a donation to the author if you find the program useful. Any search engine should soon come up with a few sites that offer this program as a free download. Ccleaner is actually rather more than a Registry checker, and it offers other features such as one that offers similar facilities to the Windows Disk Cleanup facility. Here we will only consider its use as a Registry checker and fixer.

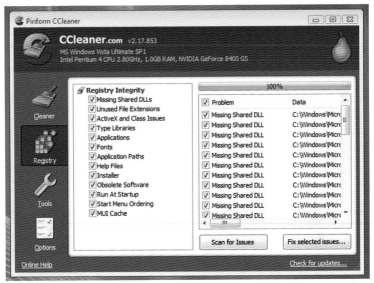

Fig.2.4 The scan has produced a scrollable list of errors

Once running, and with the Registry button selected in the right-hand section of the window, Ccleaner provides a list of things that can be checked (Figure 2.3). All the checkboxes will be ticked by default so that all the tests are carried out, and it is probably best to leave things this way. Operate the Scan for Issues button to start the checking process, which will probably take a minute or three. If any problems are found, and they usually are, a scrollable list will be produced in the right-hand panel of the window (Figure 2.4).

A brief description of each problem is given, and there is a checkbox for each entry. All the checkboxes are ticked by default, but you can remove the tick if there is a problem that you would prefer the program to leave untouched. Operate the Fix Selected Issues button when you are ready for the program to go ahead and make the changes to the Registry. You may be asked to confirm some changes (Figure 2.5), and it is just a matter of operating the Fix Issue button to confirm that you would like the change to be made. Operate the Fix All Selected Issues button if you would prefer to have the program proceed without asking your permission again.

Of course, any program of this type has its limitations. If it finds reference to a nonexistent DLL file in the Registry it cannot reinstate the missing

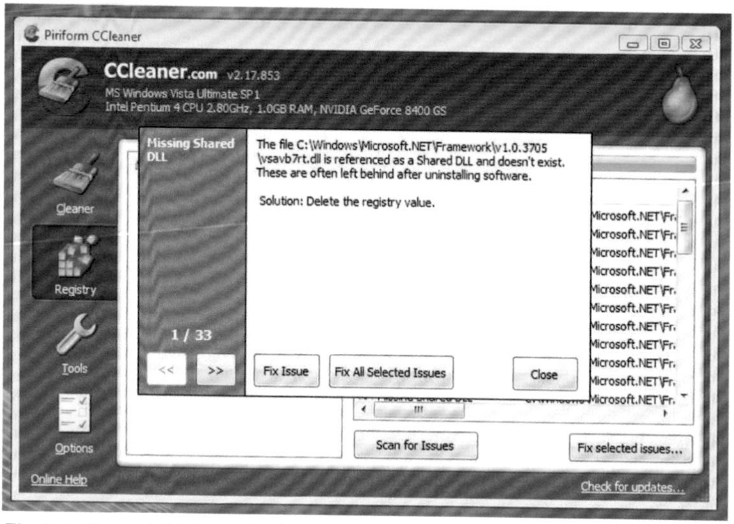

Fig.2.5 You might be asked to confirm some changes

file, so it takes the alternative course of deleting the reference to it. The missing file is probably not needed any longer, and its reference in the Registry is probably something that an uninstaller has failed to deal with properly. If the file is still needed and its absence results in an application program failing to work properly, reinstalling the application should reinstate the file and cure the problem.

Start-up problems

I think it is fair to say that modern versions of Windows are less prone to start-up problems than those of yesteryear. To some extent this is due to Windows, avoiding problems in the first place, and damaging a modern Windows installation is far more difficult than it was in the days of Windows 95 and 98. Also, a modern version of Windows will take in its stride, things that would have brought older versions to a complete halt. Of course, this is not to say that a modern Windows installation cannot go wrong and prevent the computer from booting properly. It can and does still happen, but it is far more rare than in the past.

It is a common mistake to blame Windows for any problem that prevents the computer from booting correctly. There are numerous possible reasons for a computer failing to boot properly, many of which are nothing whatever to do with the operating system. The first task is to determine whether the problem is caused by a hardware fault or the operating system. The most important factor here is whether the computer gets as far as the operating system or fails at some earlier stage in the start-up process. Before booting into Windows, a computer will go through a series of simple checks to ensure that the hardware is all functioning correctly. This is known as the POST (power-on self-test), and there will usually be some on-screen messages or a splash screen during this period. It is only once this testing procedure has been completed that the computer looks for a disc drive that contains the operating system and then tries to boot into that system. There is no point in looking for a problem with the operating system if the computer stalls before it actually reaches that stage.

Even if the computer does actually reach the boot stage, the problem could still be a hardware fault. If the boot process does actually start but then falters, it is virtually certain that there is a problem with the Windows installation. However, if things grind to a halt with an error message stating that no suitable boot disc was found, it is likely that the problem is due to a faulty disc drive rather than a faulty Windows installation on that drive. If the problem is due to a fault in the Windows installation, the damage might be so severe that no easy fix is possible.

A good initial test is to go into the Setup program that can usually be accessed by pressing a certain key once the POST has been finished but prior to the computer trying to boot into the operating system. The key used to access the setup program varies from one computer to another, but it is often the Delete key or the F2 function key. At the appropriate time in the start-up process there will usually be an on-screen message telling you which key to press in order to access this program. Once into the Setup program it is the standard CMOS section that is required. This should list all the computer's disc drives, and there is certainly a hardware problem if one of the drives is absent from the list. However, it does not necessarily mean that all is well if all the drives are listed correctly.

A drive will usually be listed as present and correct provided the Setup program can communicate with the controller circuit in the drive. The drive mechanism itself could be faulty or even totally inaccessible, but its entry will still appear properly in the list of drives detected by the Setup program. Where a drive is not listed it is quite likely that it has become totally unusable and that its contents will be lost. There are emergency recovery services that will attempt to retrieve lost data on a faulty drive, but these are too expensive for most users, and there is never any certainty that all the data on the disc will be recoverable. It is better to avoid the need of such services by always making at least one backup copy of any important data. Of course, the lack of an entry for a drive does not necessarily mean that it is completely useless, and in many cases it is just a very simple fault such as a lead that has come adrift and is not making proper electrical contact.

Hardware faults go beyond the scope of this book, so we will assume here that the computer starts to boot into Windows, and that it then either stalls completely or seems to take an eternity to finally reach the point where the computer is running the operating system properly and is in a fully usable state. Matters are certainly much easier if the computer does eventually make it into Windows, even if it does take 15 or 20 minutes to get there! It is then possible to use the built-in facilities of Windows and third party utilities in an attempt to find the cause of the problem.

The problem could be due to a problem with the Registry, and using a program such as Ccleaner to locate and fix Registry problems might help. However, with most Windows problems the built-in System Restore facility is probably the best place to start. I have used this to fix numerous problems with Windows, from disappearing broadband Internet connections to PCs that take 20 minutes to boot-up but then run perfectly. It should not be necessary to manually switch on this facility, because it is usually activated by default when Windows is installed.

System Restore was introduced with Windows ME, and is much the same on subsequent versions of Windows. It is designed specifically to deal with problems in the operating system. It should not be confused with the Backup and Restore programs that are used to deal with hard disc failures and to prevent data from being lost. The purpose of System Restore is to take the system back to a previous configuration that worked. If there is a difficulty with the current configuration, taking the system back to a previous state should cure the problem. It does not matter whether the difficulty is a greatly extended boot-up time or all your Desktop icons disappearing. Whatever the nature of the problem, provided it is caused by a change to the operating system, using System Restore should take the computer back to a state where it works normally.

System or program files that have been deleted or changed since the restoration date are returned to their previous state, and any files that have been added are deleted. Strictly speaking, System Restore is a program that will work around operating system problems rather than fix them. It will often provide a quick fix, but you have to be careful not to reintroduce the problem. It is only fair to point out that it does have one drawback, which is that it requires a fair amount of hard disc space. It

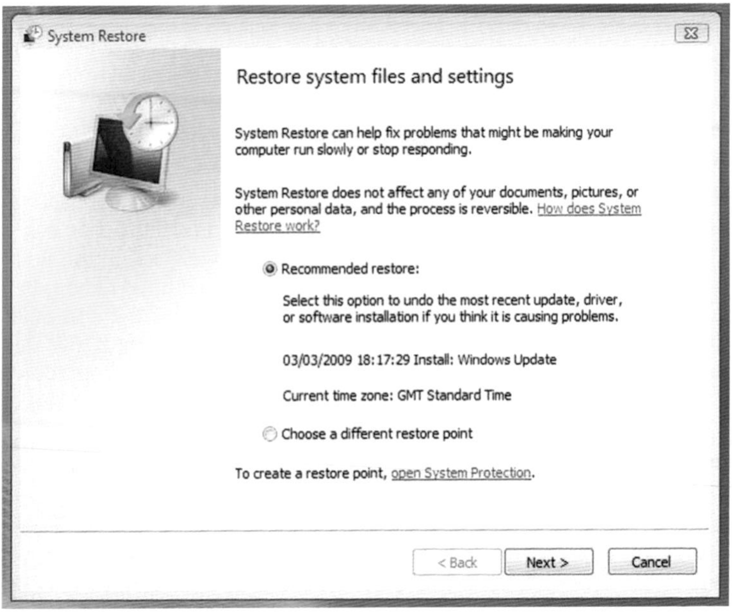

Fig.2.6 You can opt to use the recommended restore point or choose your own

needs a minimum of 300 megabytes (0.3 gigabytes), and could use up to 15 percent of a disc's capacity. It is a price that is well worth paying though, especially with a modern PC that has a huge hard disc drive. Even if (say) a 750 gigabyte drive loses 15 percent of its usable capacity by using System Restore, even with the operating system and various programs installed, this would still leave something like 600 gigabytes free for data storage.

Restore points

The general idea is to periodically add new restore points so that if something should subsequently go wrong with the operating system, it can be taken back to a recent restore point. Incidentally, Windows adds restore points periodically, so it is not essential to routinely add your own. The main reason for adding your own restore points is that there is increased likelihood of problems occurring. The most common example of this is adding a restore point prior to installing new software. If anything should go horribly wrong during the installation process, going back to

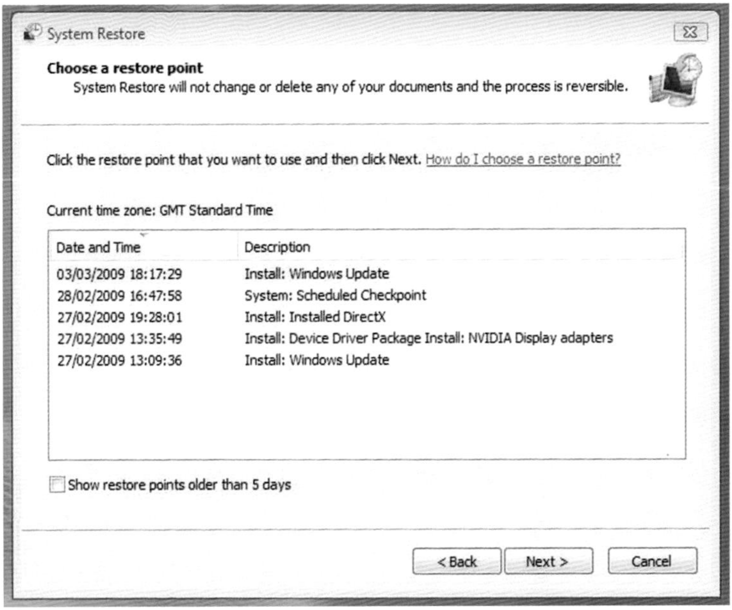

Fig.2.7 This window enables a restore point to be selected

the restore point should remove the rogue program and fix the problem with the operating system. You can then contact the software publisher to find a cure to the problem, and in the mean time your PC should still be functioning properly. It is also worth adding a restore point prior to adding or removing new hardware. This provides a way back to normality if adding or removing the device drivers has dire consequences for the Windows installation.

When going back to a restore point the program should remove any recently added programs, but it should leave recently produced data files intact. Of course, with any valuable data that has not been backed up already, it would be prudent to make backup copies before using System Restore, just in case things do not go according to plan. The program itself does provide a way around this sort of problem in that it does permit a restoration to be undone. In the unlikely event that a valuable data file should vanish "into thin air" it should be possible to return the PC to its original configuration, backup the restored data, and then go back to the restoration point again. System Restore only backs up and restores system and program files, so it is highly unlikely that it would be responsible for data files going "absent without leave".

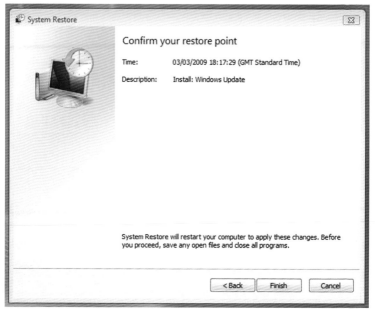

Fig.2.8 Left-click the Finish button to use the selected restore point

The System Restore facility is launched by going to the Start menu and then selecting All Programs – Accessories – System Tools – System Restore. In the System Restore window (Figure 2.6) there are two radio buttons that enable either the recommended restore point to be used, or one of your own choice to be selected. The window changes to look something like Figure 2.7 if you opt to choose a restore point. A list of available restore points is provided in the main panel, but only those produced within the last five days are shown by default. This is usually adequate, but it is merely necessary to tick the checkbox near the bottom of the Window if you need to go further than five days. Having selected a restore point, or if you use the recommended point, operating the Next button produces a window like the one shown in Figure 2.8, where you have to confirm that the restore point that is about to be used is indeed the correct one.

If all is well, operate the Finish button to get things under way. The restoration process will probably take at least a few minutes, and it will certainly involve the computer restarting. It is therefore a good idea to save all data and exit any running applications prior to using the System

Restore facility. Eventually you should end up with the computer back at the Windows Desktop, complete with a message to confirm that the operating system has been taken back to its state at the appropriate

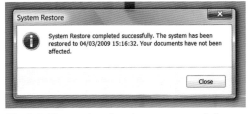

time and date (Figure 2.9). It is then a matter of trying the computer to determine whether the problem has been banished or is still present. It is probably worth trying an earlier restoration point if the problem has not been removed, possibly going back to a date well before the time when you first noticed that all was not well.

System Restore will remove most problems, but bear in mind that it does have limitations. The main one is that it will only deal with damage to the operating system. It cannot deal with problems in application programs, fix hardware problems, or deal with any errors in the operating system that have been there from the start. System Restore is unlikely to deal with problems caused by viruses or other malware, because these programs are designed to attack the system in a way that blocks simple solutions. Consequently, they will usually have to be dealt with using the normal techniques and anti-malware software.

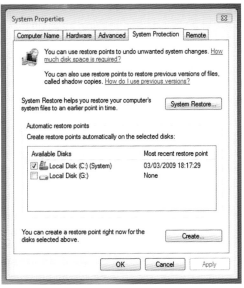

Fig.2.10 The System Protection window

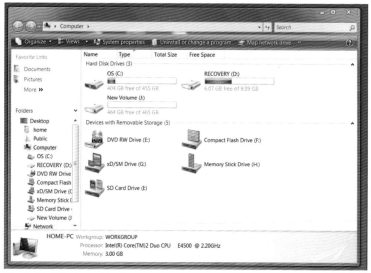

Fig.2.11 Windows Explorer has gone straight to the Computer section, and has listed all the computer's drives

Once you are sure that the system is clear of the infection it is a good idea to switch off the System Restore feature to remove all the restoration points and the disc data associated with them. This removes the possibility of using System Restore and finding that the malware has been reintroduced to the system. In order to switch off this feature it is a matter of first going to the initial System Restore window (refer back Figure 2.6), and operating the Open System Protection link near the bottom of the window. This launches the System Protection window (Figure 2.10), and here the protection for a drive can be switched on or off by adding or removing a tick from its checkbox. Note that there is usually no point in using this feature for anything other than the boot drive, which will usually be drive C. System files are not usually stored on the other drives, and activating System Restore for them would simply waste disc space.

Having switched off protection for drive C and exited the System Protection window, go straight back to it and reintroduce the protection for this drive. It will then be available if a problem should occur later on, but initially there will be no earlier restore points to return to. It is for this reason that it is important to ensure that the system is clear of any infections and running well prior to switching off the System Restore feature. Note that you can manually add a restore point at any time by

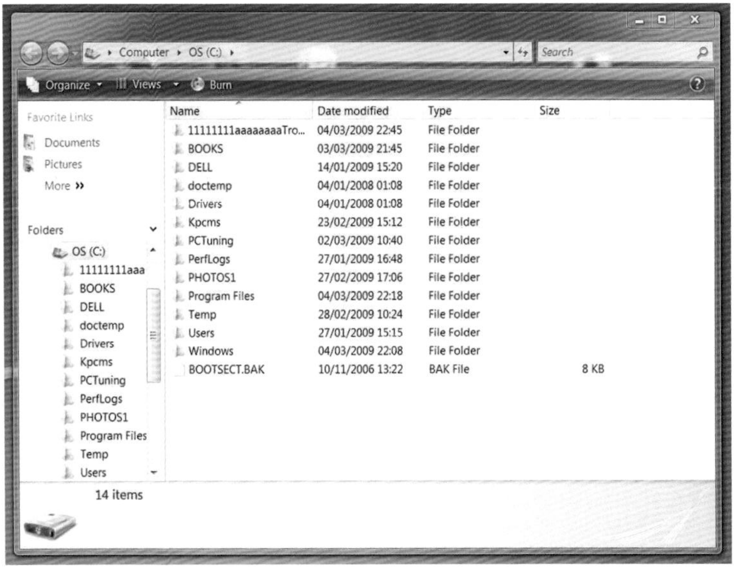

Fig.2.12   Taking things a stage further by going straight to a particular drive (drive C in this example)

going to the System Protection window and operating the Create button near the bottom of the window.

Computer shortcut

A common complaint about modern versions of Windows is that they try to force you to do things the Microsoft way rather than being free to "do your own thing". Perhaps the most obvious example of this is when you run Windows Explorer. On doing so you are provided with a directory tree down the left-hand side of the screen, but it is not like "the good old days" when you had the drives and their folders represented here. With any modern version of the program you are provided with folders such as Desktop, Downloads, and Documents, which are the ones Microsoft thinks you should use to store your data. Simply putting your own folders in place and doing things your own way is not the approved approach to things.

Of course, many users do not bother with the preinstalled folders, and instead generate their own folder structures and store data in the way that works best for them. A slight annoyance with this approach is that your folders are not immediately accessible when Windows Explorer is run. You have to scroll down until Computer appears in the left-hand panel, and then double-click this entry to produce icons for all the installed disc drives in the main panel.

The easy way around this is to drag the Computer entry onto the Desktop, which will produce a shortcut for it on the Desktop. Double-clicking the icon for this shortcut will "cut to the chase" and immediately produce Windows Explorer complete with entries for all the drives (Figure 2.11). You can take things a stage further and drag the entry for a drive to the Desktop. This produces a Desktop shortcut to that drive, and double-clicking the shortcut launches Windows Explorer, which will show the folders in the root directory of the drive (Figure 2.12).

Noise

A few years ago it was not uncommon for it to sound a bit like a jet plane taking off when a PC was switched on! There were the likely sources of this noise:

1.   **The cooling fan in the power supply unit (PSU)**

2.   **The cooling fan on the processor's heatsink**

3.   **The cooling fan on the graphics card**

4.   **General cooling fans on the computer's case**

5.   **Hard disc drives**

The amount of noise contributed by 2, 3, and 5 was usually quite low, since the sources were to some extent shielded by the computer's case. Most of the noise usually came from 1 and 4, with the former tending to be by far the noisiest of the various sources.

Thankfully, modern computers tend to be far quieter. With the popularity of the Windows Media Center and similar software, "silent running" is essential for many users. It is hard to enjoy music, films, etc., if you can barely hear the sound above the general hubbub from the computer itself! It is likely that something has come loose if a modern PC that is normally quiet suddenly starts to make "buzzing" sounds. The power supply is held in place by four screws on the rear panel of the case (Figure 2.13), and tightening these might help. Similarly, any cooling fans fitted directly on the case are usually fixed in place by four screws, and it is worth checking that these are reasonably tight.

Do not simply disconnect any fans that are noisy. Doing so will almost certainly lead to something in the computer overheating and a costly

Fig.2.13 The four screws circled in red are the ones that hold the supply in place

repair, or the computer's built-in protection features might prevent it from starting up. Sometimes a previously quiet fan becomes noisy due to dust getting into the mechanism. It might be possible to cure this problem by switching off the computer, disconnecting it from the mains supply, cleaning away the dust, and then reconnecting the supply and switching on again. In most cases it is necessary to replace the fan, preferably with a good quality type that is guaranteed to provide a low noise level.

With an old PC that has always been noisy it might be possible to obtain a worthwhile reduction in noise by replacing any cooling fans on the case with new low-noise types of the same size. In general, most of the noise comes from the power supply unit, and the only way of obtaining a worthwhile reduction in noise is to replace it with a quiet type. Note that it is not just a matter of obtaining any modern PC power supply and fitting it in place of the original unit. Firstly, the new unit must have an adequate power rating, and a 450 watt unit should be adequate unless the PC is something like a large tower unit with numerous disc drives. Secondly, the connectors on the new power supply must match those on the old unit. If this proves to be difficult, it will probably be possible to obtain adaptors that enable the power supplies connectors to be used with any older types used on the computer's main board or drives.

Physically swapping the power supply for a new one is not usually too difficult, but it is probably best to have the job done professionally unless you are reasonably conversant with computer hardware. The various power output leads must be disconnected from the main board and the disc drives. Note that the leads that go to the main board have locking connectors, and that it is not just a matter of tugging on them until they pull free from the board. There is a little lever on the connector, and this must be pressed inwards to free the connector. The supply is normally held in place by the four screws on the rear panel referred to earlier, and internally it usually clips onto the case. With the old supply removed it is then just a matter of reversing the process in order to fit the new unit and get it connected to the main board and drives.

Laptop battery life

Probably the most common complaint about laptop and notebook PCs is their battery life, or perhaps that should be their lack of battery life. Despite the improvements in battery technology and the built-in power saving features of portable PCs, the battery life per charge is often just two or three hours. There is no way of greatly extending this time, but you can improve battery life to a limited extent by doing the right things. You can also avoid doing things that tend to greatly reduce the battery life and prevent even the expected two or three hours per charge from being obtained.

In general, the more processing your laptop does, the shorter the battery life. Switching off any unnecessary processes running in the background might help. Using something like an MP3 player program while you work will reduce the battery life. Playing a DVD probably represents the most effective way of running down the battery, as it requires intensive processing and uses the motor in the DVD drive.   It is better to use a separate player and only use the laptop for word processing, spreadsheets, or whatever.

Most portable PCs automatically reduce the screen brightness when the battery is used as the power source. It is better if you avoid the temptation to manually increase the brightness. In fact it is better if you use the computer in fairly dark conditions and further reduce the screen brightness. However, do not reduce the brightness so much that you have to strain your eyes to see the screen properly.

With a typical laptop PC there is little scope for removing unnecessary hardware, since the hardware specification is usually limited to the bare essentials. However, there might be something that is not really needed. Most laptops have a wi-fi adaptor fitted as standard, and no doubt most people actually use this facility. If you do not need it though, switching it off or even removing it from the computer altogether will reduce battery drain. If you do need the adaptor, only have it switched on when it is actually in use. Remember that USB gadgets will draw power from the PC unless they have their own battery or mains power supply. It is therefore best to disconnect any USB devices unless they are actually in use, or have their own power source.

The built-in power management facilities of the computer will put it into some form of power saving mode if you do not operate the keyboard or pointing device for a short time. You do not have to wait for this to happen though, and with Windows Vista it is possible to place the computer in Sleep or Hibernation mode using the same menu that is used when shutting down the computer. The Hibernation mode gives the greatest power saving. It places the contents of the computer's memory onto the hard disc so that it can be restored when the computer is reactivated. This enables the computer to carry on where it left off, but in the meantime it consumes no significant power.

The only slight drawbacks are that stopping and starting the computer takes longer with the Hibernation mode than it does with the virtually instant Sleep mode, and the Hibernation mode does not seem to be totally reliable with all PCs. It is probably best to test it a few times before using this facility in earnest. Always save any unsaved work before placing the computer into Hibernation.

In order to get the full capacity from a laptop battery it used to be necessary to fully discharge the battery before recharging it. Modern laptop batteries do not have this problem, and you can simply top up the battery whenever there is a chance to recharge it. However, most manufacturers seem to advise users to fully discharge and then fully recharge the battery from time to time. This helps to keep it in good condition and working at full capacity.

There is a limit to the number of times that a battery can be charged and discharged, but a modern battery is likely to be good for at least one thousand charge/discharge cycles. Even so, with regular use it is likely that the battery will start to fail after a few years and will have to be replaced. Bear in mind that most rechargeable batteries are not good at retaining a charge even when they are new. If a laptop has not been used for a week or three it is a good idea to recharge the battery to ensure that it is fully charged again.

Of course, the best way of extending battery life is to use the mains adaptor whenever possible. Always take the adaptor when you take the laptop on your travels, and use it at every opportunity. Remember that using the adaptor does not only prevent battery drain, it also recharges

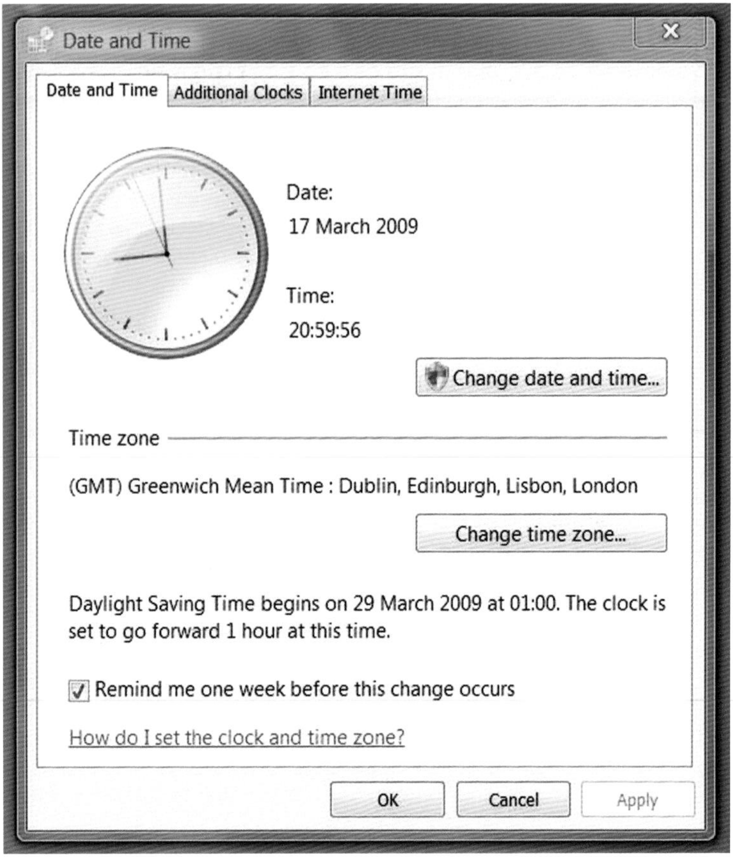

Fig.2.14 The Vista Date and Time window

the battery, although at a slower rate than when the computer is not in use.

Cannot play DVDs

Many PCs are supplied complete with Windows Vista, but in many cases it is Windows Vista Home Basic that is provided. This is sufficient for most purposes, but it is a budget option that lacks some features that are present in the more expensive versions, and with Windows XP. One

Fig.2.15 This window enables the time and date to be set

of these is that there is no built-in decoder for playing DVDs, and an error message is obtained if you try to play one. The ability to play DVDs is a standard feature with the Home Premium and Ultimate editions, but a DVD player program is needed when using the Home Basic edition.

CMOS error

This is a problem that mainly afflicts PCs that are several years old, and the user is made aware of it by an error message that appears before the computer starts to boot into Windows. The message is something along

Fig.2.16 The CMOS back-up battery is normally a large "button" cell

the lines of "CMOS checksum error – set time and date". The "CMOS" referred to here is some memory that is used to store information used by the BIOS (basic input/output system). This information includes such things as the amount of memory installed, details of the computer's disc drives, and numerous parameters connected to memory timing, the ports, and so on. This information is stored in some special memory that will not get a severe case of amnesia when the computer is switched off, or non-volatile RAM (NVR) as it is sometimes called.

This memory is often of a type that will actually lose its contents when the power is switched off, but a small battery is used to power the memory during the periods when the computer is not in use. As the memory consumes minute power levels it does not significantly drain the battery, which should therefore last for at least a few years. Eventually the battery will fail though, and the error message mentioned previously is then produced when the computer is switched on. Part of the computer's POST (power-on self-test) routine does some clever mathematics to ensure that the contents of the memory have not been corrupted, and the message is produced when an error is detected here. The problem could be due to a hardware fault, but it is usually the result of the back-up battery going flat and the contents of the non-volatile memory being lost.

A modern BIOS will automatically detect the computer's hardware and use sensible figures in the database stored in the non-volatile memory. Consequently, the loss of the original data is not usually a serious problem. Suitable parameters will be used anyway, and the computer should be perfectly usable. The computer does not know the current time and date though, so these have to be entered by the user. This can be done via the BIOS Setup program, but it is easier to use the facilities built into Windows. Go to the Classic version of the Control Panel and double-click the Date and Time icon. This produces a window like the one in Figure 2.14, and operating the "Change date and time" button produces the pop-up window of Figure 2.15. Here the date and time can be set using the normal Windows methods of control.

Of course, setting the correct date and time makes the computer fully usable again, but it does not cure the problem. It will lose the contents of the non-volatile memory when the computer is switched off, and the date and time then have to be set once again. The remedy is to replace the battery, which is usually a button cell fitted in a simple holder somewhere on the main board (Figure 2.16). The battery should be marked with its type number. Some of these batteries are widely available, but others have to be obtained from a computer store or battery specialist.

Up-to-date drivers

Many of the problems encountered with PCs are due to problems with the driver software. Practically every piece of hardware in a PC system, whether it is an internal part of the PC or a peripheral gadget, will not work with Windows or application programs unless suitable drivers have been installed. In theory there should be no problems with driver software, since numerous drivers are installed as part of the operating system, and any piece of PC hardware is supplied complete with drivers for recent versions of Windows. The problems stem from the fact that driver software is very complex, and the hardware manufacturers often seem to have problems producing driver software that is totally free from bugs. There can also be difficulties caused by conflicts between two items of hardware. These conflicts are irrelevant to most users, but can cause major problems if you just happen to be using the two relevant items of hardware.

It is advisable to check that the driver software you are using is the most up-to-date that is available, and one way of doing this is to go to the manufacturers' web sites yourself to check for updates. The alternative is to let Windows do the searching for you. This is done by going into Device Manager and finding the entry for the piece of hardware that you would like to update. Device Manager can be run via its icon in the Classic version of the Windows Control Panel. Once in Device Manager, double-click the entry for the relevant piece of hardware in order to launch its properties window. Alternatively, right-click its entry and choose Properties from the pop-up menu. Select the driver section of the Properties window (Figure 2.17) and then operate the Update Driver button.

A new window will then appear on the screen, and this offers the choice of having Windows search the computer and the Internet for a newer driver, or just the computer. In this case it is the Internet that we wish to

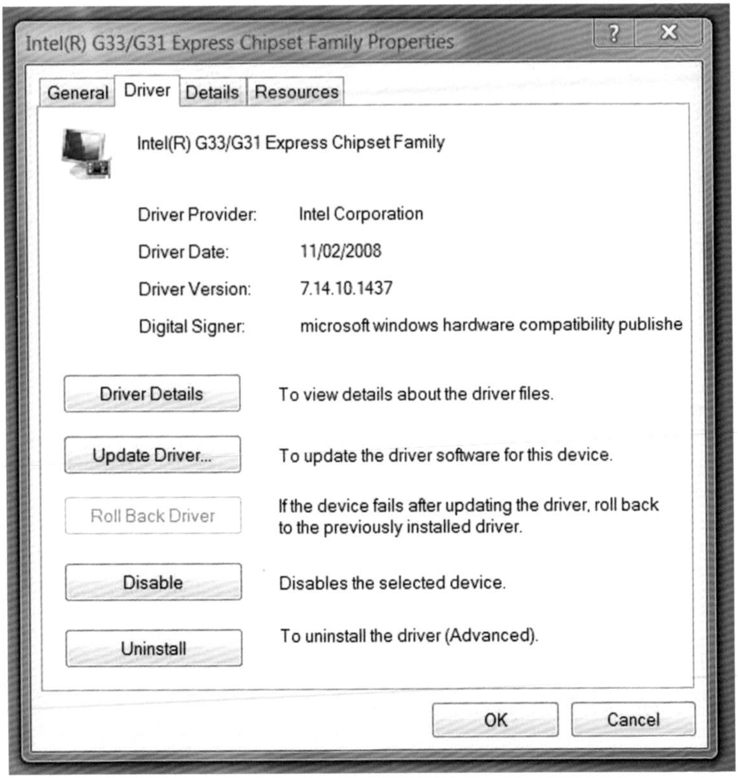

Fig.2.17 Select the Driver section of the Properties window

search for a new driver, so it is the upper link that is activated. There will then be a delay while the search is made. You will be asked if you wish to go ahead and install the newer driver if something suitable is found. It is then just a matter of going ahead with the usual installation process, which is unlikely to require any input from the user. In this example a more up-to-date driver was not available, as explained by the information window of Figure 2.18.

Although updating driver software should always provide benefits such as extra features, better performance, or bug fixes, it can very occasionally make matters worse. This is often the result of some sort of resources conflict between the updated device and some other item of hardware in the computer. This type of thing is often missed when the driver software is at the testing stage, because the computers used for the testing did

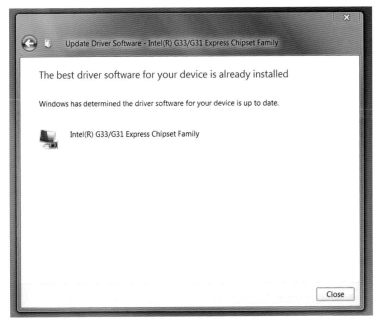

Fig.2.18 In this example, a more up-to-date driver could not be found

not have the precise hardware configuration needed to cause the conflict. Of course, mistakes are sometimes made, and the problem could simply be due to the hardware manufacturer's software writers getting it wrong.

Anyway, it is possible to cure the problem if new driver software makes things worse rather than better. The Drivers section of the hardware's Properties window includes a Roll Back Driver button, and operating this enables the new driver software to be removed and replaced with the previous version that you used. Of course, this button will only be active if there is an earlier version that Windows can revert to. There is also an Uninstall button, which enables the existing drivers to be removed but does not replace them with anything. The drivers have to be installed from scratch if this option is used.

Legacy software

The subject of problems encountered when using old peripherals with Windows Vista is covered in the next chapter, but it is not only old hardware that can be problematic when used with modern PCs.

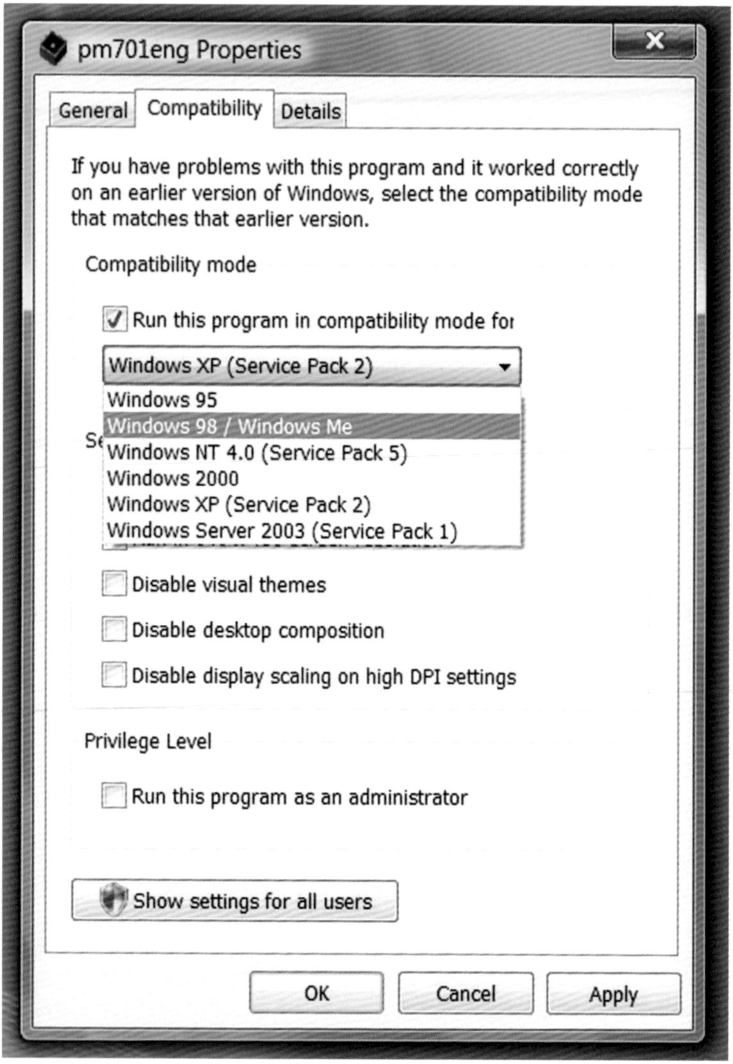

Fig.2.19 Several compatibility modes are available

Programs that were written for earlier versions of Windows will not necessarily run flawlessly when used with Vista. Some types of software, and particularly certain types of utility such as system checkers and

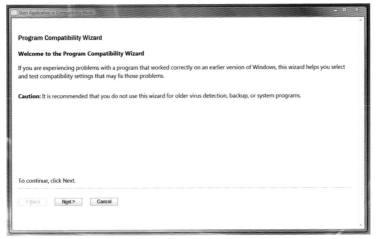

Fig.2.20 The initial window of the Program Compatibility Wizard

antivirus programs, are not recommended for use on anything other than the version of Windows they were written for. Using these programs on a computer that is running under an unsuitable version of Windows could result in damage to the operating system.

Such restrictions do not apply with most application software though, and it is usually fine to use older programs with later versions of Windows. Compatibility issues are quite likely to arise though, principally with the very old and the more complex programs. Windows Vista has the ability to run programs in compatibility modes that try to use the same operating conditions as earlier version of Windows. This is fine in theory, but it is only fair to point out that there is no guarantee that it will give satisfactory results with any given program. Sometimes it produces an improvement, while in others it seems to make no difference. It is certainly worth trying this feature when older programs fail to run smoothly under Windows Vista.

In order to run a simple program in a compatibility mode it is a matter of finding the program file using Windows Explorer, and then right-clicking its entry and choosing Properties from the pop-up menu. Operate the Compatibility tab when the Properties window appears, and then tick the "Run this program in compatibility mode for" checkbox. The menu immediately beneath this then becomes active, and it is possible to opt for compatibility with various Windows operating systems from the past (Figure 2.19). There are some further options available, such as using

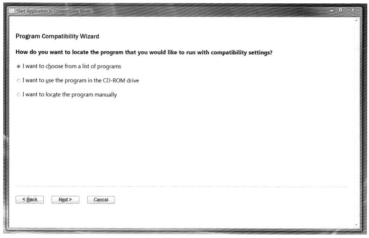

Fig.2.21 There are three ways of selecting the required program

very basic video modes, but it should only be necessary to use these when trying to run software from the dim and distant past. This approach is only suitable for a very simple program, and it is mainly used with something like a Setup program that refuses to run properly, making it impossible to install the main program. With something of this type it is easy to locate the program file and set it to the required compatibility mode.

With the more complex programs the best approach is to use the Program Compatibility Wizard. Strangely, there is no way of running this wizard via the Windows menu structure. Instead, you have to operate the Start button, choose Help and Support from the menu items in the right-hand column, and then enter a suitable text string such as "program compatibility wizard" into the Search textbox. Press the Enter key, and windows should respond with a list of results that has "Start the Program Compatibility Wizard" at or near the top. Operating this link does not actually start the wizard, but instead produces an information page where there is a link that really will launch the Program Compatibility Wizard (Figure 2.20). This starts by warning against using a compatibility mode with certain types of program, such as antivirus software, which should only be used with their intended versions of Windows.

Provided you are not trying to use an inappropriate type of program, operate the Next button to move things on to the next step. The new version of the window gives a choice of three ways to select the correct

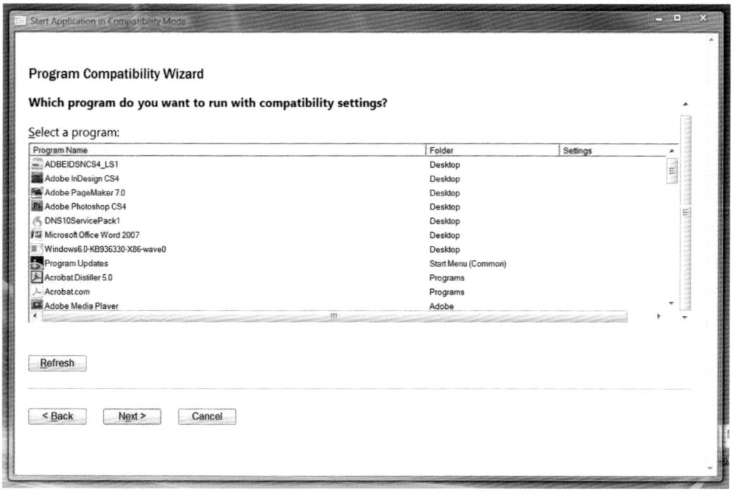

Fig.2.22 Use this window to select the required program

program (Figure 2.21), and the default option of choosing from a list of programs is usually the easiest. It is only necessary to use one of the others if the program has not been installed in Windows for some reason,

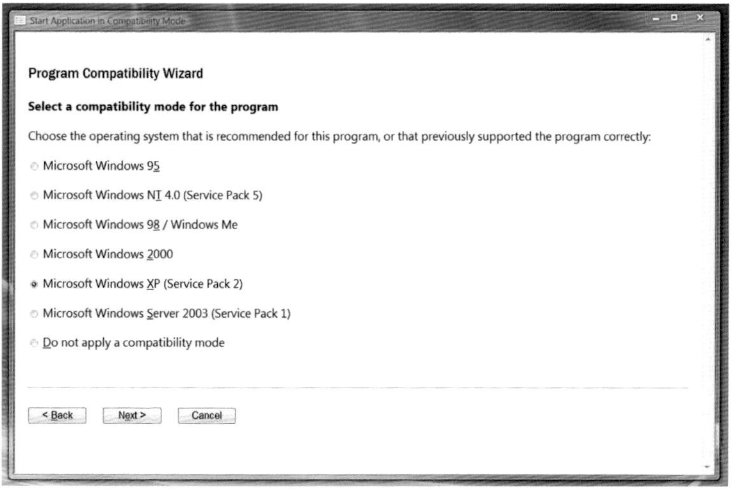

Fig.2.23 Here the required compatibility mode is selected

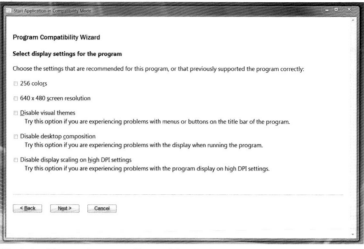

Fig.2.24 The options on offer at this window are only needed when running some very old programs

and it is not included in the list. Any major item of software should be installed in Windows, and should therefore be included in the list.

Fig.2.25 This information screen shows the options that have been selected

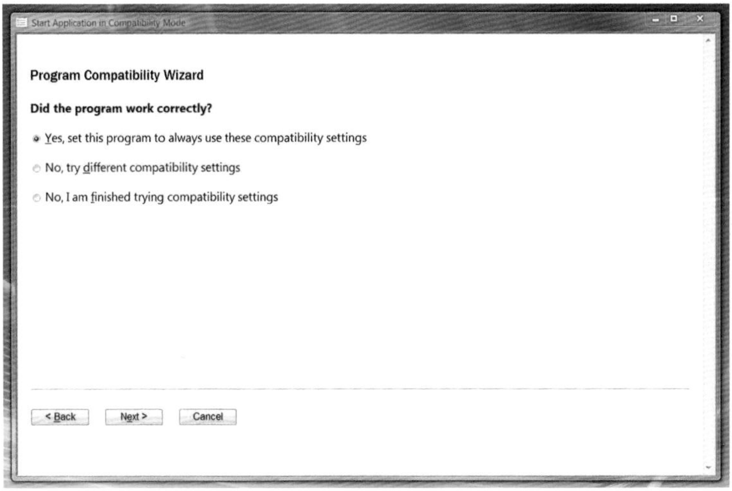

*Fig.2.26 The existing settings can be retained, or a different
compatibility mode can be tried*

There will be a short delay if this option is used, but after a brief scan of
the hard disc drive the wizard should produce a list of the installed
programs (Figure 2.22). Select the appropriate program by left-clicking
its entry, and then operate the Next button. This changes the window to
the one shown in Figure 2.23, where the radio button for the required
version of Windows is selected. Moving on to the next window (Figure
2.24), there are options for things such as low video resolution and colour
depth, but the checkboxes can be left blank if none of these are needed.

At the next window there is the option of running the program as an
administrator, and a brief explanation of why this might be necessary.
Unless you are trying to run software in one of the appropriate categories,
such as a program designed to run under Windows 95 or 98, leave the
checkbox blank. Finally, you get the information screen of Figure 2.25,
and it is then time to operate the Next button and test the program using
the selected compatibility mode. Having tested it, the Program
Compatibility Wizard then gives the option of trying different settings, or
leaving things as they are (Figure 2.26). You do not have to continue
using a compatibility mode, and normal operation can be restored by
running the wizard again and opting not to use a compatibility mode
when the window of Figure 2.23 is reached.

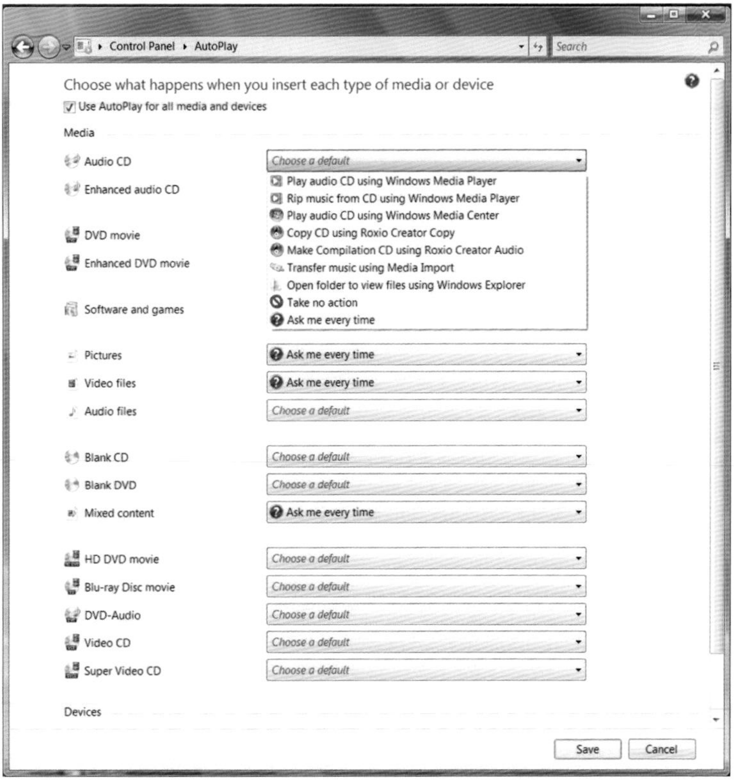

Fig.2.27 The window that is used to control the auto-play facility

Auto-play problems

Perhaps the auto-play feature for CD and DVD drives has never worked exactly as you would like it to, or perhaps it used to work fine but then you installed a new piece of media software and it has not been the same since. The problem with many programs is that they try to take over the computer when you install them. The fact that a program is ill-suited to certain tasks will not prevent the installer from doing its best to make that program the default for all of those tasks. Neither will the fact that there is already a much more suitable alternative program already installed make any difference. If allowed to, an installer will often do its best to be the automatic choice for everything that it can handle, even if it can only handle it badly.

This is something where prevention is better than cure, and during the installation process there is usually the option of choosing the changes that the installer will make to any default settings of the system. When installing software there is a tendency to take the easiest path, and simply accept a typical installation using whatever settings the installer uses by default. This is probably a mistake when installing any new software, but it definitely pays to be more careful when dealing with any form of media related software. If in doubt, it is probably best to opt for no changes to be made.

There are really two separate but related areas where things tend to go awry, and these are the auto-play and default program features. There are really two sets of default programs, which are those used to open some form of media or data file, and those used to play discs of certain types when the auto-play feature is active. The two sets are controlled independently, and we will deal with the auto-play feature first. The default settings can be altered by going into the Classic version of the Windows Control Panel and double-clicking the AutoPlay icon. This produces the control window of Figure 2.27 where the auto-play facility can be switched on or off via the checkbox near the top left-hand corner of the window.

If it is active, a series of menus enable the required action for each type of disc to be set. The available options will vary somewhat, depending on the software installed on the PC. Note that it is not necessary to have a default action for each type of disc, and that each menu gives the option of having no action taken for that particular type of disc. Another point to bear in mind is that the selected action will be used for any removable disc that contains the appropriate type of file. The selected actions for music and pictures will therefore be applied if a Flash card containing music or picture files is inserted into a card reader.

Default programs

The auto-play feature determines what, if anything, happens when a removable disc of some kind is placed into a drive. The Default Programs feature is used to assign a program to a particular type of data file, and that program will be automatically run and used if a data file of that type is double-clicked in a file browser such as Windows Explorer. It does not matter whether the data file is on a fixed (hard) drive or on a removable type. Double-clicking its entry in a file browser will launch the relevant program and open the file in that program.

The program defaults are largely set up for you when application software is installed on the computer. If you install Microsoft's Word word-

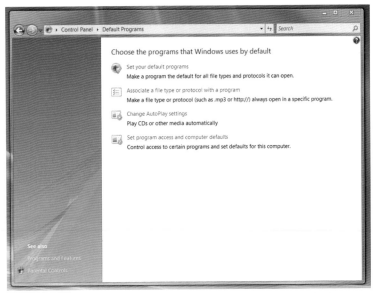

Fig.2.28 Four options are available from this window, but only the upper two are normally of interest

processing program for example, it will be used as the default program for documents in one of the normal Word formats, such as DOC and DOCX documents. Most problems occur when you have two or three programs that can use the same general file types. For example, many programs are capable of using files such as the JPG and TIFF image types. The program that ends up as the one used by default to open these files might not be the one that you would prefer to use.

The default program settings can be altered by going to the Classic version of the Windows Control Panel and then double-clicking the Default Programs icon. This produces the window of Figure 2.28 where there are four options. It is only the upper two that are of interest here, and the top one enables a program to be set as the default for any type of file that it can handle. This is a rather "hit and miss" way of doing things, and it is generally better to use the next option down, which enables a particular file type and program to be linked. Using this option produces a window like the one of Figure 2.29, where all the known file types are listed on the left, with the corresponding default programs shown on the right. Where "Unknown application" is shown in the Current Default column, this simply means that there is no default program for that type

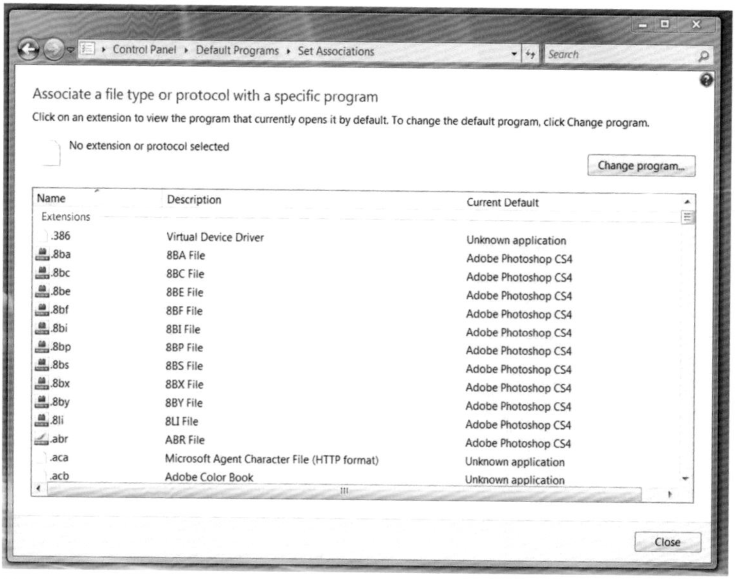

Fig.2.29 All the known file types are listed here. The list is very long, but it is in alphanumeric order

of file at present. The list of file types is extremely long, but it is reasonably easy to find the ones you require because it is in alphanumeric order.

Having found a required file type it is just a matter of left-clicking its entry to select it, and then operating the Change Program button near the top right-hand corner of the window. This produces a pop-up window similar to the one in Figure 2.30, showing an icon for each of the installed programs. Of course, the programs listed here will be the ones installed on your particular PC, and will not be the same as the set of programs show in Figure 2.30. There is a Browse button that can be used to launch a file browser so that you can search for the program file if the program you require is not listed. This will not normally be necessary, and it is probably best not to try this option unless you are sure you know what you are doing.

In order to assign a program in the list as the default it is merely necessary to left-click its entry to select it, and to then operate the OK button. The program should then be listed as the default back at the main file associations window. This process is repeated for any other file types that you wish to change to a different default program.

Fig.2.30 This window has an icon for each of the installed programs

Peripherals and the Internet

Lead astray

In the early days of personal and home computers you tended to connect peripheral devices to your computer more in hope than expectation. Although the ports were supposedly standardised, in reality manufacturers were quite prepared to bend the rules and "do their own thing". Getting even the more "run of the mill" peripherals such as printers and modems to work with your computer was often problematic, and in a few cases it was impossible to get the peripheral gadget to work exactly as it should. Fortunately, things have improved over the years, and the USB interface, albeit after a slow and difficult start, has eliminated many of the problems that were commonplace in the past. Of course, in the computing world nothing is guaranteed to work perfectly at the first attempt, and the occasional problem can still occur.

Legacy ports

These are ports that were once used as the main means for a PC to communicate with peripheral gadgets such as modems and printers. The main legacy ports are the RS232C serial, parallel (printer), and PS/2 (mouse and keyboard) types. These days there are more modern ports available for this type of thing, such as the USB and Firewire types, and new computers often lack some of the legacy ports. In fact the computer I am using to write this piece does not have any legacy ports at all, and this is rapidly becoming the norm for Desktop PCs. It has been the norm for laptop computers for some years now.

There is obviously a problem if you have an old peripheral with a serial or parallel port that you wish to use with a new PC that does not have

Fig.3.1 A serial port adaptor that plugs into a USB port

legacy ports. Wherever possible it is probably best to replace the peripheral with a modern device that has a USB port. However, there is a potential solution in cases where it is not practical to replace the peripheral gadget. It is possible to obtain adaptors that enable serial or parallel devices to be used via a USB port. A USB serial port adaptor is shown in Figure 3.1. These do not work well in all situations, but in most cases a unit of this type will permit the peripheral to be used with a modern PC.

Bear in mind that getting an old gadget connected successfully to a PC and actually getting the computer to work with the gadget are two different things. There are several potential problems, but the main one is that the old gadget will only work with a new PC if there is suitable driver software available. Driver software for older versions of Windows is usually of no use with the current versions. Most manufacturers of PC peripherals do not produce modern drivers for use with older equipment that they consider to be obsolete. If an old peripheral requires special driver software in order to work properly with Windows, using an adaptor to connect it to a modern PC running Windows Vista will probably be a pointless exercise.

This problem is less likely to occur if you use a USB adaptor to enable an old PS/2 keyboard or pointing device to be used with a modern PC. In most cases it is just a matter of connecting everything together properly, switching on the computer, and then waiting while the PC boots up and Windows loads the standard driver software. I am typing this piece into a PS/2 keyboard connected to the computer via a USB adaptor, and everything works as it should. Problems are only likely to occur with some of the more fancy keyboards that have numerous extra keys that can provide clever features when supported by the appropriate utility software. The extra features will only work if the software is compatible with Vista.

Audio CD problems

In the early days of audio CDs the manufacturers were keen to promote the idea that the discs themselves were virtually indestructible, and would still play perfectly after all manner of ill-treatment. Practical experience suggests that CDs are indeed far more durable than vinyl discs, but if the playing surface is marred they will probably tend to "skip", or fail to play at all if the damage is severe. Provided the damage is not really bad and the disc does not have some form of copy protection, it is often possible to use a program such as Nero to copy the disc. The error detection and correction facilities of the program will try to fill the gaps in the data from the original disc, and generally smooth things over.

How well this works depends on the extent and nature of the damage to the original disc. It will not necessarily be possible to copy the disc, so it is best to do a dummy run before trying to make the copy. Most disc burning programs have the option of doing a test run before actually writing anything to a disc, and using this facility can avoid unnecessarily wasting CD-Rs. Where the disc can be copied, at the very least it should be possible to play the copy without the track skipping or repeating problems of the original. With luck, the correction facility will fill in the gaps without leaving any audible gaps or glitches.

Note that this ploy will only work with audio CDs, where slight errors in the copied data are not too important. It will not give improved results with program and data discs, where the copy will be a faithful duplicate of the original, complete with the same flaws. Some drives are better than others at reading "iffy" discs, so it is worth trying other PCs if a disc cannot be read properly using the PC you try first. If you can find a PC that will read a problematic disc in error-free fashion, use that computer to make a copy of the disc. The copy should then be readable in any computer that has a CD drive in reasonable working order.

Various CD cleaning products are available, and these are usually very effective at removing stains and minor blemishes from the playing surface.

Unfortunately, they are unlikely to be of any help with a disc that has deep scratches or other major physical damage. It pays to bear in mind that CD-R discs are much less tough than factory pressed CDs. With a "proper" CD the sheet of metal that contains the data is sandwiched between and protected by two pieces of transparent plastic. A normal CD-R disc has one piece of transparent plastic with the light-sensitive coating on the upper side, and then the maker's label on top of this. In other words, on one side of the disc the label provides the only protection for the data stored in the light-sensitive layer. If the label becomes chipped or scratched, the light-sensitive layer will almost certainly be damaged as well, with a consequent loss of data.

Noisy discs

If you place a disc into a CD-ROM or DVD drive, and it sounds rather like a thunderstorm as soon as the disc starts to rotate, do not assume that the drive has had a catastrophic failure. The most likely cause of the problem is that you have put a second disc in the drive without removing the first disc. Another possible cause is that you have used the last CD-R from a bulk pack of the type that has the disc on a long spindle. There is usually a clear plastic disc at the bottom of the pack, and this often sticks to the disc at the bottom of the pile. Pandemonium results if you fail to notice this and put the two discs in the drive. Fortunately, although it sounds as though the drive and the discs are self-destructing, in most cases they all seem to come through the experience largely unscathed.

Paper jams

Of the common computer peripherals, I think it is fair to say that printers are probably the most troublesome. In the early days of home computing the main problem was actually getting the printer connected to the computer in a suitable fashion. Better standardisation of modern computer ports has removed this problem. Things should go well initially provided you make sure that the driver software you are using is the latest version for the operating system in use, and the manufacturer's installation instructions are followed correctly. Matters are not always straightforward once you start printing.

The paper getting jammed in printers was a common problem in the early days of personal computing, and it is an aspect of computing that seems to have made little progress over the years. Most of the problems with early printers centred on fanfold paper used with tractor feeds. This type of paper feed is little used these days, and it is automatic sheet feeders that are responsible for most of the difficulties with modern printers. The usual problem is that several sheets of paper stick together. There is no major problem when a couple of sheets occasionally stick together. You simply get the odd blank page mixed in with the printed pages. Things are more serious if more than about three or four sheets stick together, since this can "gum up the works" and produce a serious paper jam. This problem can usually be avoided by running your thumb down each edge of the block of paper before loading it into the printer. Thumbing through the paper should separate any sheets that have stuck together at the edges.

The wrong paper setting is another common cause of paper jams. Setting the printer for use with thin paper and then using thick paper, film, or envelopes is the less dire mistake. It could result in a paper jam, but in most cases the feed mechanism will simply fail to load anything. Results are likely to be less happy if the printer is left at a setting for thick media and then used with thin paper. I had an inkjet printer that our cats found irresistible as a bed, and they would frequently knock the paper thickness lever from its thinnest setting to the thickest. If no one noticed that the setting had changed, a paper jam would soon follow. About 20 or 30 sheets of paper would start to feed into the printer, but the feed mechanism would jam with the paper about 25 percent of the way into the printer.

Unfortunately, the printer would do its best to continue feeding the paper through, printing away on the same strip of paper which soon became drenched with ink. This is typical of paper jams caused by an incorrect paper setting. In trying to force a block of paper through the printer, the feed mechanism can self-destruct. In the case of my inkjet printer, parts of the mechanism became distorted, and eventually it could only be used with single sheets of paper. It is therefore important to avoid paper jams in general, and this type of jam in particular.

Freeing jams

When a paper jam occurs it is essential to switch off the printer as quickly as possible and disconnect it from the mains supply. This prevents the paper feed mechanism from doing any more damage, and makes it safe to start removing the jammed paper. Switching off the printer will get Windows confused, with the printer suddenly failing to respond. An error message might appear on the screen. It is advisable to use the Cancel option and terminate the print job, if the message includes this option.

Fig.3.2 This window shows all the installed printers

Alternatively, go to the Classic version of the Windows Control Panel, double-click the Printers icon, and then in the Printers window (Figure 3.2) double-click the icon for the printer you are using. This will produce a small window that includes an entry for the stalled print job. Right-click the entry and then select Cancel from the pop-up menu (Figure 3.3). With some of the pages damaged, there is no realistic prospect of finishing the current printing job. Instead, it is a matter of salvaging as many of the completed pages as possible, and then printing the other pages. The Print window permits a specified range of pages to be printed, so there is no need to print all the pages again if the initial pages from the first print run are all right.

It is prudent to consult the printer's instruction manual before trying to remove the paper that is stuck in the printer. This should offer some guidance about the easiest way of removing the paper, and it might include some warnings about things that you must not do in order to avoid damaging the printer. In general, the best way to remove the paper is to pull it back out of the printer, rather than trying to get it to go through the printer following the normal paper path. Trying to move the paper forwards is likely to jam it more tightly, making matters much worse. Get the best grip you can on the paper and then pull it firmly and steadily. Usually, this will slowly but steadily unwind the paper until it pulls free.

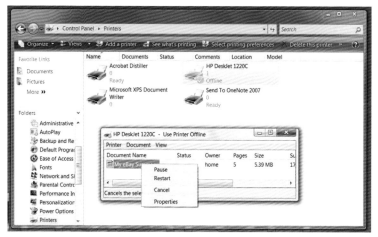

Fig.3.3 Choose the Cancel option to remove the stalled printing job

Jerking the paper will probably result in it tearing, leaving you relatively little to get hold of. The slow but steady approach is more likely to have the desired effect.

Test pages

It can be useful to print test pages in situations where the printer is connected up and raring to go, the printer's drivers are installed, but the printer will not actually print anything. A test page can usually be printed during the Windows installation process, and it is a good idea to choose this option as it will make any problems clear from the outset. The page produced varies from one printer to another, but typically there is a small graphic and a message at the top of the page. Further down the page there might be something like a colour test section and some technical information about the printer's drivers and installation. It is usually pretty obvious if things have gone wrong. In most cases nothing at all will be printed, or the printer will produce garbage.

It is possible to print the test page without going through the installation routine. The first step is to go to the Classic version of the Windows Control Panel and double-click on the Printers icon. Once into the Printers window, right-click the icon for the appropriate printer and choose Properties from the pop-up menu. This brings up the Properties window for the printer, and this window varies from one printer to another, but

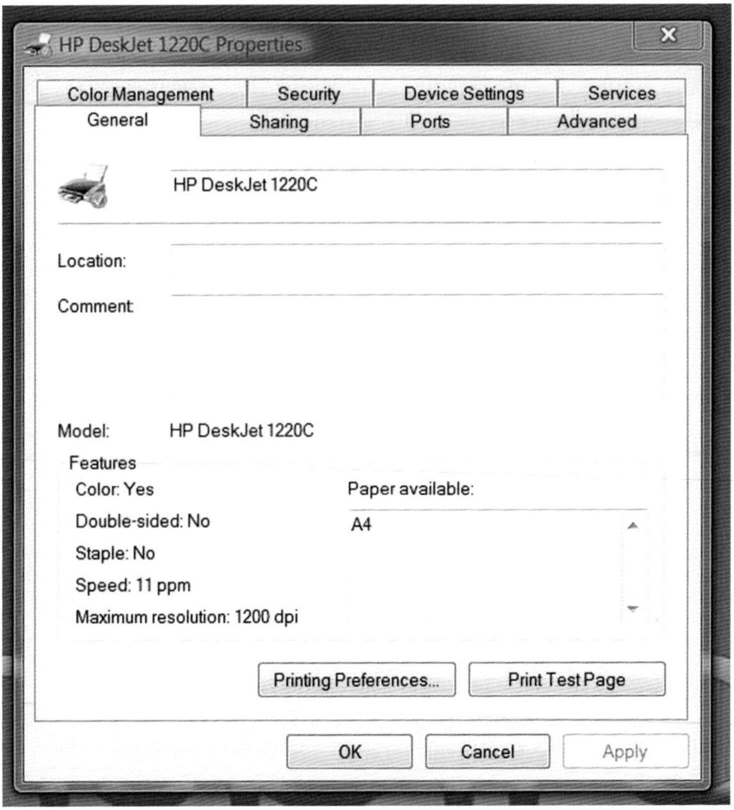

Fig.3.4 The options under this tab include one to print a test page

under the General tab there should be a button marked "Print Test Page" (Figure 3.4). Operating this button should result in the test page being printed and the window of Figure 3.5 appearing.

If all is well, left-click the Close button to clear the window from the screen. There is nothing wrong with the printer drivers, the printer, or the connecting cable, if the page is printed correctly. Try printing from a Windows application again, but this time ensure that the correct printer is selected. You can change the default printer by going to the Printers window, right-clicking on the printer you wish to set as the default unit, and then selecting Set as Default Printer from the pop-up menu. There is a tick shown against the default printer's icon in the Printers window, and in Figure 3.2 it is the HP DeskJet 1220C that is set as the default printer. The standard Windows printing facilities enable the required printer to be selected when printing documents, so make sure that the correct printer is selected when printing from

Fig.3.5 Operate the Close button if the page printed correctly

application programs. This setting will override the default setting in the Printers window.

Check the other settings if the correct printer is selected and the printer is still not functioning correctly. Is the page range something valid, or are you trying to print pages that do not exist? Does the paper size match the paper that you are actually using? Modern printers tend to have numerous options available, and these can be accessed via the Properties button when in an application program's Print window. The settings available here clearly have to match the facilities of the printer, and they are therefore different for each model. However, there is usually a section that controls the resolution, and there may be other settings that govern the paper type, use of toner or ink saving, and others aspects of the print quality. Is the printer producing poor quality results because it is set to a low-resolution mode so as to use as little ink or toner as possible?

When the test page is printed properly but an application does not produce any output from the printer, there is a strong possibility that it is the application rather than Windows or the printer that is at fault. The easy way to check this point is to open another application, produce a quick test document, and then try to print it. If the printer works properly with all but one application, clearly that application is faulty.

There could be a bug in the program, but in most cases the fault is due to a file being damaged or accidentally removed. Reinstalling the program over the original installation will often repair the damage. The uninstaller for the program might include a repair option. If that does not have the desired effect, try uninstalling the program, shutting down the computer, rebooting it, and then installing the application again. There is probably a bug in the program if neither method of reinstallation cures the problem. It is then a matter of contacting the program's publisher to see if a software fix is available.

Failed test

If the test page is not produced properly you can operate the Close button anyway, and continue to search for the problem yourself. Alternatively, you can operate the link that activates the Windows support system. In Windows Vista this results in the Printing Troubleshooter being launched (Figure 3.6). To some extent Windows troubleshooters try to locate problems by making their own investigations, but they mostly rely very heavily on input from the user via a series of simple questionnaires. As one would expect, the initial window gives a number of options that broadly define the problem. Subsequent windows attempt to reduce the number of possible causes until the precise nature of the problem is found.

Self test

Many printers have a built-in testing facility that prints a test page when a certain combination of control buttons is pressed, or when the appropriate menu item is selected. Where appropriate, the printer's instruction manual will give details of how to produce the test page, and it will also show what the correctly printed page should look like. This method of testing is different to getting Windows to produce a test page. The Windows method checks the printer drivers, the printer port, the connecting cable, and the printer itself. The entire system is functioning correctly if the test page is printed correctly, and the fault must be in the applications software.

The built-in test page is stored in a memory chip inside the printer, and a correctly printed page shows that the printer is largely operational. However, this type of checking does not involve the PC or the connecting cable, and the test page will normally be produced even if the printer is not connected to a computer. A correctly produced test page probably means that the problem lies in the computer or the data cable, but it is important to realise that this type of testing does not involve the input port of the printer. Consequently, there could be a fault in the printer's interface circuitry.

If the whole system seems to be free from faults, the self-testing procedure produces the correct result, but it is still not possible to print from Windows, a fault in the printer's interface is the most likely cause of the problem. Ideally, the printer should be tried with another computer and data lead. A lack of response when the printer is driven from the computer almost certainly means that the interface circuitry is faulty. Perfect results using the new cable and computer probably indicates a fault in the original data lead or the first PC's port hardware. Try the printer with the first computer again, but this time use the second printer cable. The original printer cable is faulty if this clears the problem, and the port hardware is faulty if the problem persists.

Slow printing

Many users suspect that there is a fault with their printer because it fails to meet the printing speeds quoted by the manufacturer. When looking at printing speeds it has to be borne in mind that

Fig.3.6 The first page of the troubleshooter

these usually assume ideal operating conditions, which might be difficult to reproduce in practice. In fact, independent tests on printers often fail to get close to the quoted printing speeds. Therefore, the figures quoted by manufacturers have to be taken with the proverbial "pinch of salt".

Also, bear in mind that printing speeds are usually dependent on the type of printing that is undertaken. The obvious example is the difference in print speeds of a typical inkjet printer when used for monochrome text printing and colour photographs. An inkjet printer might produce several pages per minute when printing text, even if used in the highest quality mode. Printing large colour photographs is likely to reduce the print speed to so many minutes per page rather than so many pages per minute. Many inkjet printers take 10 to 20 minutes to produce full-page colour photographs at the highest quality setting.

The file format also seems to have some influence on printing speeds, particularly when using a printer that relies on Windows and the computer to do most of the processing. The Adobe PDF (Portable Document Format) is one that seems to make most printers grind along at a much slower rate than normal. One reason for this is probably that PDF tends to be used for complex pages containing a mixture of text and graphics, which is a combination that often produces relatively slow printing speeds. Anyway, it certainly takes a large amount of processing to turn PDF files into printed documents, and most printers do the job more quickly if they are driven from a powerful computer equipped with plenty of memory. With any complex pages there is a risk that the printing speed will be limited by the speed of the PC rather than the physical limits of the printer, especially when using an old PC equipped with a relatively small amount of memory.

Printer cables

Most computer peripherals are supplied complete with all the necessary cables, but printers are an exception. Every printer should come complete with a mains cable, but it is unusual for a data cable to be included. For most users this is not a problem, since the printer will be a replacement and the old lead can be used with the new printer. There is a potential problem here in that modern printers have a USB interface whereas older ones have a parallel (Centronics) interface. Some printers have both types of interface, but the vast majority of modern printers have only a USB interface. In this situation a parallel printer lead will therefore be of no use, and a USB lead should be obtained when purchasing the printer. An ordinary A to B lead is needed to connect a printer to a PC, and a lead of this type should cost very little.

The lack of a parallel port on modern PCs can be a problem if you need to use an old printer with a new PC. As pointed out previously, the easy solution is to use a USB port with a parallel port adaptor. Most modern adaptors of this type provide an excellent emulation of a genuine parallel port, and once installed into Windows can be used in exactly the same way as a normal parallel port. Most units of this type look like a printer lead having a USB plug at the computer end and a Centronics connector at the printer end. There is some sophisticated electronics in one of the connectors though, and the unit is powered from the USB port. Strangely, an adaptor of this type sometimes costs less than an ordinary parallel printer lead!

Streaky printing

Laser printers sometimes produce pages that contain pale vertical streaks that run the full height of the printed part of the page. This effect tends to be more noticeable on photographs than on text, but it gradually becomes worse until it is obvious on any page content. The usual cause is that the toner powder is not evenly distributed across the full width of the paper. There should be no problem initially provided you follow the manufacturer's installation instructions, and gently shake the cartridge backward and forward a number of times before fitting it in the printer. This distributes the toner reasonably evenly, and with a lot of toner present in the cartridge there should be no faint areas on the printed pages.

As the toner is used up, it is inevitable that streaky printing will eventually occur. Any parts of the cartridge where the toner is a bit shallow at first will start to run out of toner first. The toner will be used quite quickly in some parts of the cartridge while other parts will have a much lower rate of consumption. As parts of the cartridge start to run out of toner powder, the streaks start to reappear on the corresponding parts of the printed pages.

Most printer manufacturers recommend that the toner cartridge be replaced when the streaking starts to appear. However, there is usually a fair amount of toner left in the cartridge, which can therefore be given a new lease of life by repeating the shaking treatment. With one of the smaller personal laser printers, there is no need to remove the cartridge. The whole printer can be shaken backward and forward. This is clearly impractical with anything other than the smallest laser printers, and in most cases the cartridge will have to be removed, shaken, and then refitted. A surprising number of additional pages can often be squeezed out of a cartridge using this simple process, particularly when the toner was not evenly distributed in the first place.

The shaking can be repeated when the streaky pages start to appear a second time, but there is a limit to the number of times that this process will work. It becomes more difficult to spread out the powder as the amount in the cartridge reduces. Eventually there will be an insufficient quantity to produced good quality printouts, and the cartridge will then have to be replaced or refilled.

Colour problems

Undoubtedly the most common printing problem I am asked to sort out is inkjet printers that produce totally inaccurate colours. In most cases there is no fault at all, and it is just that one of the ink reservoirs has run out. Inkjet printers operate on a four-colour system known as CMYK (cyan, magenta, yellow, and black). Cyan, magenta, and yellow are the three primary colours, and they are mixed to produce other colours. Black is added to give darker colours, and less ink is used to give paler colours. The paper, which must be white in order to produce the correct colours, effectively adds the white that gives the pale colours.

The black ink is used for printing text, and this type of printing will not be possible if the black cartridge runs out of ink. Colour printing will still be possible, but without the black ink there will be no dark colours. Black and white text printing can proceed normally when the colour cartridge has run out of ink, as can the printing of monochrome images. However, colour printing will produce some odd looking results.

One of the three coloured inks will run out before the other two reservoirs run dry, and this will affect any colours that require the missing primary colour. This can leave some parts of a colour photograph looking remarkable normal, while other areas are heavily affected. Up-market inkjet printers sometimes use more than three colours in an attempt to obtain greater colour accuracy, and the result of one colour running dry is then less drastic. It will still produce very noticeable errors in the colours though.

Where the problem is due to an exhausted ink cartridge, replacing it should cure the problem. If a new cartridge does not make any difference, then one of the tubes connecting the ink cartridge to the print head has become blocked, or part of the print head has become clogged. Either way, the printer needs to be professionally serviced. Some printers, including all the Hewlett Packard DeskJet printers, have the print head built-into the ink cartridge. This method has its detractors, but it has the big advantage that you get a new print head when you fit a new cartridge. Fitting a new cartridge therefore cures any ink blockage problems.

A major repair on an inkjet printer often costs more than the value of the printer. It is then more economic to buy a new printer rather than have the old one repaired. There are kits available that can be used to clean the ink paths when a blockage occurs, and it might be worthwhile trying one of these before discarding a printer that is otherwise in good condition.

Stripy printing

Printouts having horizontal stripes are a common problem with inkjet printers. Most printers of this type require a calibration process to be carried out before they are used, and many need this process to be repeated each time that a new ink cartridge is fitted. These stripes are very likely to occur if the calibration is omitted or not carried out properly. It is possible for a printer to creep out of calibration, so it is worth repeating this process if the stripes start to emerge when the printer has been in use for some time.

Thin white stripes across the pages normally indicate that some of the nozzles in the print head are not firing ink droplets. In most cases this occurs because the ink cartridge is nearing exhaustion. It is unfortunate if replacing the cartridge does not cure the fault, because this means that the nozzles are blocked and an expensive repair is needed.

Spotty printing

When an inkjet printer produces printouts that contain random spots of ink, it is usually the result of an earlier paper jam or other fault that resulted in ink from the print head getting into the paper feed mechanism. The easiest way of clearing away the ink is to repeatedly feed a sheet of paper through the printer. It should gradually mop up the ink and restore clean printouts. If the spotting occurs when there has been no previous mishap, check that the cartridge is installed properly. Any ink in the cartridge compartment should be mopped up, and the ink cartridge must be replaced if the problem persists.

The problem might simply be due to an excessive flow of ink. With printers that have the print head and ink reservoirs combined, this problem should be cured by replacing the ink cartridge. An expensive repair might be needed if the cartridge and print head are separate units. However, before seeking a repair, make sure that you are using a suitable type of paper, and that the printer is set for use with that type of paper. Some types of paper require relatively little ink, and will often produce spotty and smudgy results if the printer is set for use with the wrong type of paper.

Laser printers can also have problems with spotty printouts, but the same pattern of dots usually appears on every page. Typically, the spots appear slightly lower on successive pages, eventually moving back to the top again. Looking at things in highly simplified terms, the electrostatic image is normally "drawn" onto plastic film by the laser beam, and then transferred to the paper. The toner powder is then attracted to the appropriate parts of the paper and heated so that it melts and glues itself in place. When dust finds its way onto the plastic film it upsets the normal operation of the printer and tends to produce corresponding specks on the printouts.

With some laser printers the photosensitive drum is not a consumable and it cannot be replaced easily. The cost of repair is usually very much more than the value of the printer. Fortunately, this type of printer seems to be largely immune to the dust problem. Realistically, if it should occur there are only two options available. Put up with it or buy a new laser printer. Many laser printers do have a user changeable drum, but the replaceable type is not necessarily very drum-like. In catalogues it is usually called something like a "photo-conductor". With a photo-conductor that is well used, the obvious solution is to replace it. As these units are quite expensive, you may well be reluctant to replace one that has received relatively little use. Depending on the design of the printer, it is sometimes possible to remove the photo-conductor, clean it, and then refit it in the printer. The cleaning has to be done carefully though, as it is easy to add more dust than you remove. Lens cleaning kits for cameras are useful for this job.

USB power

Using USB ports tended to be problematic when this type of interface was introduced, and for some time afterwards. Fortunately, these problems have now been solved, and using USB ports should be largely straightforward. An error message when you plug in a USB device could be due to a fault in the peripheral gadget, but it probably indicates that you are trying to do something that is beyond the capabilities of the equipment you are using. This is certainly the case if you get a message stating that the port cannot provide sufficient power to operate the peripheral device.

There are two likely causes of this problem. One is simply that you are trying to use a modern USB 2.0 device with a computer that has the original USB 1.1 specification ports. The amount of power that can be drawn from a USB 2.0 port is four times higher than the power that can be obtained from a USB 1.1 type. Some USB 2.0 gadgets will work perfectly well with USB 1.1 ports, but this is not a combination that is recommended. Using USB 1.1 devices with USB 2.0 ports is perfectly all right, since USB 2.0 ports are designed to be compatible with USB 1.1 equipment.

The other likely cause of the problem is that a passive USB hub is being used to increase the number of USB ports. A passive hub enables several USB devices to be used with a single USB port of the computer, but the power from the computer's USB port is shared amongst the ports on the hub. With (say) four ports on the hub, each one can provide only one quarter of the power that is available from a normal USB port. This is sufficient for small gadgets such as mice and other pointing devices, and is irrelevant with peripherals that have their own power source. However, it is unlikely to work with larger gadgets such as scanners.

The solution is to either plug the more power-hungry gadgets directly into a USB port on the computer, or to use a powered hub that has its own power supply and provides the full amount of power to each USB port. Note that many laptop PCs and other portable PCs have USB ports that can only provide a very limited amount of power. These must either be used with USB devices that draw little or no power from the port, or via a powered USB hub.

Microphone problems

A common problem with PC sound systems is that they function perfectly for some time, but fail when you eventually try to record sound via a microphone, use a voice recognition system, or use some other application that requires a microphone to be used. On the face of it there is no problem, with headsets that include a microphone on offer at low prices from any computer store. All PCs, including laptops and notebooks, seem to include standard miniature jack connectors for use with these headsets. Unfortunately, plugging the two jack plugs into the correct sockets on the PC does not always provide good results. The headphone side of things is not usually a problem, and a line or loudspeaker output will usually suffice if there is no output socket specifically intended for headphones. It is connecting a microphone to a PC that tends to be problematic.

This is not usually due to a fault in either the soundcard or the microphone. The problem is due to a lack of proper standardisation with PC microphone inputs. The problem is usually due to incompatibility between the microphone and the audio system. Due to the lack of true standardisation, a microphone that works perfectly well with one card might give no signal at all when used with another. The microphone problem stems from the fact that the microphone inputs of early SoundBlaster cards, and many of the compatible cards of a similar age, are intended for use with a carbon microphone. This is a rather crude form of microphone, as used in early telephone handsets. The audio quality of a carbon microphone is usually quite low, but the output signal is at a very high level by microphone standards. Hence, the microphone inputs of most early soundcards, and some recent ones come to that, are relatively insensitive.

Although the microphone connector on the card is a stereo 3.5-millimetre jack socket, this is normally a monophonic input. The third terminal is used to provide power to the carbon microphone, and not to provide a second stereo channel. By no means all soundcards have this type of microphone input. Some have a monophonic input with one terminal of the input socket left unused, while others do actually have a stereo microphone input.

Carbon microphones are little used with soundcards these days, and in all probability they never have been used to any extent with PCs. The normal choices at present are electret and dynamic microphones. Electret microphones require a power supply to operate, and this is often in the form of a built-in battery. However, some electret microphones are designed for use with a SoundBlaster style microphone input, and use the soundcard as the power source. Dynamic microphones do not require a power source, but often have very low output levels.

There is clearly plenty of scope for incompatibility problems when using the microphone input of an audio card. If you use a low output microphone with an insensitive input there will probably be too little audio signal to be of any practical use. If you use a microphone that requires power from the soundcard, it will only work if the card actually provides a suitable power source. This type of microphone will probably fail to produce any output signal at all if it does not receive power from the soundcard. Using a stereo microphone will clearly not give the desired result if the card only has a monophonic microphone input.

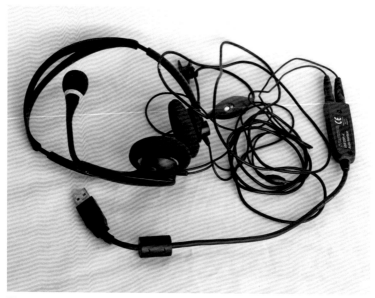

Fig.3.7 Using a USB headset can solve a lot of problems

Sorting out microphone problems tends to be difficult. In theory, it should be possible to obtain information about suitable types of microphone from the soundcard's instruction manual or the manufacturer's web site. With an integrated audio system it is the instruction manual for the motherboard that should be consulted. In practice, the information available on this subject is often sketchy to the point of being virtually non-existent. You often end up trying any microphone you can lay your hands on in the hope that it will work.

The easy solution to microphone problems is to use a USB headset (Figure 3.7). At one time these were quite expensive, but they can now be obtained at very reasonable prices. A headset of this type is really an ordinary headset, complete with the usual jack connectors, and a matching USB audio interface. The computer's normal sound system is not used at all with the headset, which has its own audio system. Good results should be obtained because the supplied headset and the USB audio interface are designed to work well together. Some of the USB interfaces include digital processing that helps to optimise results. I have certainly found USB headsets to be far better than other types when using voice recognition systems.

Contentious Internet point

One of the most common complaints in modern computing is that the actual rate at which data can be downloaded via a broadband Internet connection is far less than the speed quoted by the ISP (Internet service provider). With any form of Internet connection it has to be borne in mind that the quoted speeds are theoretical maximums, and that they are definitely not guaranteed minimums or typical figures. There can be a number of reasons for this shortfall, and there is no easy solution to most of them.

With an ADSL broadband connection your computer is connected to the Internet via a pair of ordinary copper wires that were originally designed to carry voice signals. Modern technology manages to make very good use of what is really an old-fashioned system, but a few compromises have to be made. One of these is that an ordinary ADSL connection is contended. In other words, some the connecting wires and equipment at the telephone exchange are used by more than one broadband connection. The number of broadband connections that share a single resource is called the contention ratio.

The contention ratio for a broadband connection intended for business use is relatively low, but is still likely to be 10:1 or 20:1. The figure for a home broadband Internet connection is usually more like 30:1 or 50:1. In theory, the actual connection speed of each line could be quite low at times of peak demand, since the overall bandwidth is shared by many users. The speed of each line would still be comfortably higher than a dial-up connection, and in practice there is little likelihood of even half the users using the system simultaneously. At least, I suppose it could happen occasionally for a fleeting moment, but it is unlikely that a large number of users would simultaneously download huge amounts of data.

Contention ratios have not been a major issue in the past, since the actual ratios were far lower than the guaranteed maximum figures. Also, few people were using the Internet for applications that required vast amounts of data to be downloaded. This situation is obviously changing somewhat, with ADSL broadband now being used by relatively large numbers of people, and high bandwidth applications such as downloading television programs becoming very popular. This greatly increases the chances of the actual connection speed being significantly less than the connection speed quoted by your ISP. There could be a real advantage in using an ADSL broadband connection that has a relatively low contention ratio. However, this is likely to cost very much more than a budget home broadband connection.

Cable

Note that there are no problems with contention ratios when using a cable broadband connection. The cable in this case is of the fibre-optic variety, which avoids some of the problems associated with an ADSL connection. The two cable operators in the UK have merged into a single company, and are now part of Virgin Media. Unfortunately, the cable network falls well short of covering the entire country, and in many areas it is simply not an option. Unless the cable network runs past your house it will not be possible to use this type of Internet connection. You can check whether the cable network is available at your postcode by going to the Virgin Media website and using their online checking service. This is the web address:

http://allyours.virginmedia.com/websales/service.do?id=2&buspart=search

Other factors

There are other factors than can result in reduced ADSL broadband speed. One of these is simply the distance between the user and the telephone exchange, and to some extent the quality of the electrical connection between the two also has an effect. Improvements have been made to the system over the years, but in order to achieve the higher ADSL connection speeds it is still necessary to live quite close to the telephone exchange and to have a good quality telephone connection. The only certain way to find out is to get the connection installed and then test the connection, but talking to close neighbours who use an ADSL Internet connection should give a good idea of the likely connection speed. Again, a cable broadband connection using fibre-optic cables does not have this problem. You either get the full speed or no service on offer at all.

Another important point to bear in mind is that the Internet itself is not instant. Even when using a 56k dial-up connection it is possible that the connection to the Internet will sometimes be faster than the Internet itself. The maximum rate at which data can be transferred is limited by the slowest part of the system. As Internet connections have become faster over the years, the speed of other parts of the system has become more significant. At times of exceptional demand it is possible for large parts of the Internet to slow down under the extreme loading on the available resources. A more common cause of low speeds is simply that the server at the other end of the system has more users than it can

Fig.3.8 The homepage of pcpitstop.com

comfortably accommodate. For much of the time you are waiting your turn in a queue rather than actually downloading anything.

Speed test

There are a number of web sites that will provide a free speed test, and using one of these can be helpful if you feel that your broadband connection speed is well below the sort of speed that you should be obtaining. The speed testing site used as the basis of this example is www.pcpitstop.com (Figure 3.8). In order to obtain meaningful results it is necessary to use a site that is hosted by a server that is reasonably near, and not one that is somewhere on the other side of the world. With a large distance between your PC and the test site's server it becomes more a test of the Internet than speed check for your broadband connection. In this case there is the option of using a server in London, which is only around 65km from my house, and it should therefore provide meaningful results.

Fig.3.9 The test has been completed, and the results are not bad

Operating the button for the required server brings up a new web page and then the testing begins. After a few seconds the results should appear (Figure 3.9), and you have to decide for yourself whether they are good, bad, or indifferent. In this example the broadband connection is an 8 megabit type, but the test shows that the link was only managing a little over 7 megabits per second. The upload speed also fell slightly short of the notional figure for this broadband connection. However, both speeds are actually quite good, and trying the test again produced slightly better results. Do not jump to conclusions if the tested speed is well below the figure you were expecting. You really need to make tests at various times of day and on each day of the week to determine whether there is genuinely a problem, or that a relatively slow download rate is obtained at times of high demand.

Download managers

If speed checks show that your Internet connection is working well, but downloads seem to go rather slowly and occasionally stall completely, a download manager such as FDM, Flashget, or DAP could help to speed things up. One function of a download manager is to try to make sure that the rate at which data is downloaded is as close as possible to the maximum rate that your modem supports. There are three main approaches, and one of these is to test the various sources of the file so that the fastest server or servers can be used. Another is to use settings that are likely to give optimum results when downloading large files. A program that only adjusts settings is usually called an optimiser or accelerator rather than a download manager. However, the terminology of these programs is rather loosely applied, so you need to read the "fine print" in order to determine the exact facilities provided by any programs of this genre. Frankly, tweaking a few settings is unlikely to make much difference to the rate at which large files are downloaded.

The third acceleration technique used by download managers is to use multiple threads. In other words, the download manager uses more than one connection to the server that is providing the file you are downloading. This is pointless if using a single connection enables the file to be downloaded at a rate that is close to the maximum supported by your broadband connection. It has more potential if the problem is due to a slow server that is sourcing data at (say) a tenth of the speed supported by your Internet connection. Using ten connections to the server would enable data to be extracted from the server ten times more quickly, providing a download rate at the maximum supported by your Internet connection.

In practice it is not quite as simple as that. There are inefficiencies in the system, and these will to some extent reduce the improvement obtained. Another problem is simply that some servers do not support multiple threads, making it impossible for a download manager to exploit this technique. However, where it can be used, the multiple thread technique can produce a massive increase in the download speed from a slow server.

A download manager can also be used to carry on where you left off if the connection to the server is lost. This mainly occurs with dial-up connections, which tend to be less reliable than any form of broadband Internet connection. It can also be a problem when using a wi-fi link to the modem or router. Normally there is no way of continuing with a download if the connection is lost. Establishing the connection again and continuing with the download will almost invariably result in the process starting "from scratch", and the part of the file downloaded previously will be lost. Even if there were only a few bytes of a 100-megabyte file left to go when the connection went down, the part of the file that was downloaded will be lost!

With large files and unreliable servers it may only be possible to download large files with the aid of a download manager. Without one you might never get more than half the file downloaded. In less severe instances it can still save a lot of wasted time, since you will not keep downloading the same data over and over again until the complete file is eventually downloaded in one lump. The ability to resume downloads is probably the most important one provided by download managers.

Wi-fi woes

Wi-fi enables computers to be networked without the need for any connecting cables, and it has become extremely popular in recent years. I suspect that its sudden rise in popularity is not primarily because users find it useful to network their PCs, but because wi-fi makes it easy to share an Internet connection. Many of the problems with wi-fi systems are probably due to a lack of planning. In fact most people do not seem to do any planning, and simply position everything in the system where it is most convenient from the user's point of view, rather than where it is likely to work well. Ideally there would be no problem in doing things this way, but in the real world it will often provide poor results.

When using a wi-fi system it is helpful to bear in mind that this type of radio link tends to be quite pernickety. The UHF (ultra-high frequency) radio signals used by wi-fi equipment have very short wavelengths, and this can result in signal strengths varying considerably if one of the aerials is moved a small distance. Even moving an aerial a few centimetres can produce a significant change in signal strength. One reason for this is that quite small objects in the wrong place can partially block the signal. You might occasionally find that what was a very good signal suddenly becomes a noticeably weaker one. The most likely cause is that something placed close to one of the aerials is absorbing the signal. Even someone moving slightly near one of the aerials or between two aerials can produce a dip in the signal strength.

Another problem is due to reflected signals that combine with the main signal. It is possible that the two signals will combine in a fashion that produces a boost in signal, but it is just as likely that they will have a cancelling effect, giving a reduction in the signal level. In an extreme

Fig.3.10 The aerial will not work really well at the rear of the computer

case there can be one or more "blind" spots where there is no significant signal. Again, something being moved to just the wrong place can produce a sudden decrease in the signal level.

The cure in both cases is to move the aerial in an attempt to obtain a better signal level. This should not be a problem with an external wi-fi interface that connects to the PC via a cable. With a built-in interface and some form of portable computer it might be a trifle inconvenient, but it should still be possible to move the computer slightly in an attempt to obtain a better signal. Moving the aerial is clearly going to be more difficult if it is fixed to a substantial piece of equipment such as a desktop PC or a printer. In this respect, PCI wi-fi adaptors are very restrictive, and a USB type is more versatile.

Rather than moving the entire PC and (possibly) redesigning your office to get the wi-fi link to work well, it would probably be better to get an extension cable to permit the aerial to be positioned away from the PC. Having the aerial right next to the earthed metal case of the PC is far from ideal. Despite your best efforts it may well be in amongst some

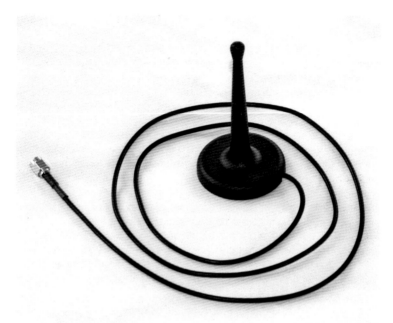

Fig.3.11 Using an aerial that connects to the computer via a short lead permits better positioning

cables as well (Figure 3.10), and these will make matters worse. The truth of the matter is that the rear of a PC is just about the worst place to have a wi-fi aerial. Moving the aerial away from the cables and the PC's case will often provide much improved results. Some PCI wi-fi adaptors are now supplied with an aerial that has a built-in stand and a lead to connect it to the PC (Figure 3.11), and practical experience suggests that these are much more likely to provide good results.

The problems are much the same with a USB wi-fi adaptor that plugs straight into the back of the PC, but there is an easy solution. A USB extension cable enables the unit to be used away from the PC and will often give much better results. Note that this does not require the usual A to B lead of the type used with printers, scanners, and most other USB peripherals. An A to A cable of the type used to link two PCs is not the right type either. These contain some electronics and are quite expensive. It is a simple and inexpensive A to A extension cable that is needed.

Internet blockage

Sometimes an Internet connection can slow down to the point that it is largely unusable. This is not anything to do with contention ratios and (or) a lack of speed because you live a long way from the telephone exchange. Issues such as these can prevent you from obtaining a really fast Internet connection, but they still leave a connection that is reasonably fast. Even if you get a connection speed of only about 512 kilobits per second, this is still about ten times faster than a good dial-up connection. It should certainly be fast enough to get complex web pages to load very quickly. If there are problems with pages taking a very long time to load and (or) frequent error messages such as "page not found", there is probably a minor hitch with your PC. There are other possibilities, and the Internet itself can virtually grind to a halt at times due to an exceptional amount of traffic. This is rare though, and the problem is usually short-lived. There could be a hardware fault at the telephone exchange or in your PC. These are both relatively unlikely though, and with a hardware fault it is usually a case of no Internet at all rather than a very slow and hesitant connection.

The usual starting point when trying to clear a "gummed up" Internet connection is to remove the temporary Internet files. The problem can be due to files in the temporary Internet cache getting the operating system confused and slowing things down instead of speeding them up. I generally use the built-in Disk Cleanup facility of Windows XP or Vista (see chapter 1) to remove the temporary Internet files, and it is a good idea to remove any other unnecessary files while using this facility.

If that does not improve matters, it is possible to use Internet Explorer to delete more temporary Internet files. From the Tools menu, choose Internet options and then select the General tab in the Internet Options window (Figure 3.12). There is a Delete button here, and operating this removes a whole range of files including cookies, your Internet history, and saved passwords. While removing such a wide range of Internet files has its advantages, and is more likely to clear the Internet connection than simply deleting the cache of temporary Internet files, it has drawbacks as well. Many of the things that happened automatically previously, such as automatically signing in at web sites, will have to be done manually. Of course, the system will soon relearn to do these things for you again, so this is not really a major drawback.

If none of this helps, try shutting down the computer, and if the modem you are using is an external type that has its own power source, such as a combined modem and router, switch this off as well. Then wait a few seconds, switch the modem back on again, and let it connect to the

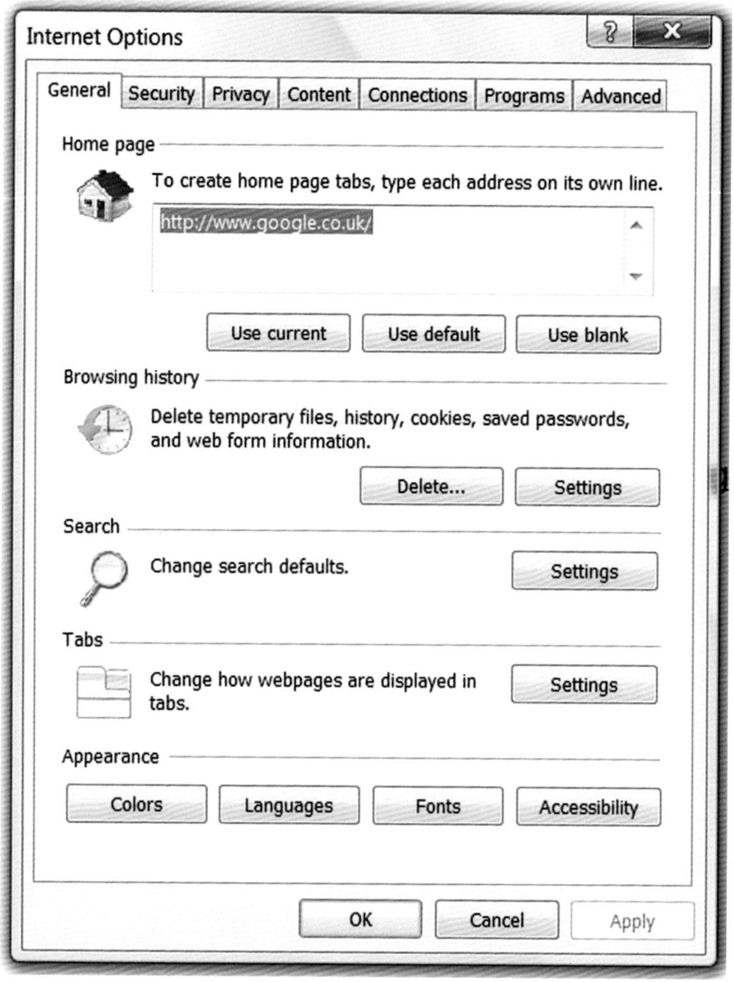

Fig.3.12 Using the Delete button erases a wide range of Internet files

Internet. Next switch the computer back on and try the Internet connection again. It might be worth resetting Internet Explorer if the Internet connection is still not performing properly. This can be done by going to the Tools menu, selecting Internet Options, and then operating the Advanced tab in the Internet Options window (Figure 3.13). Operating

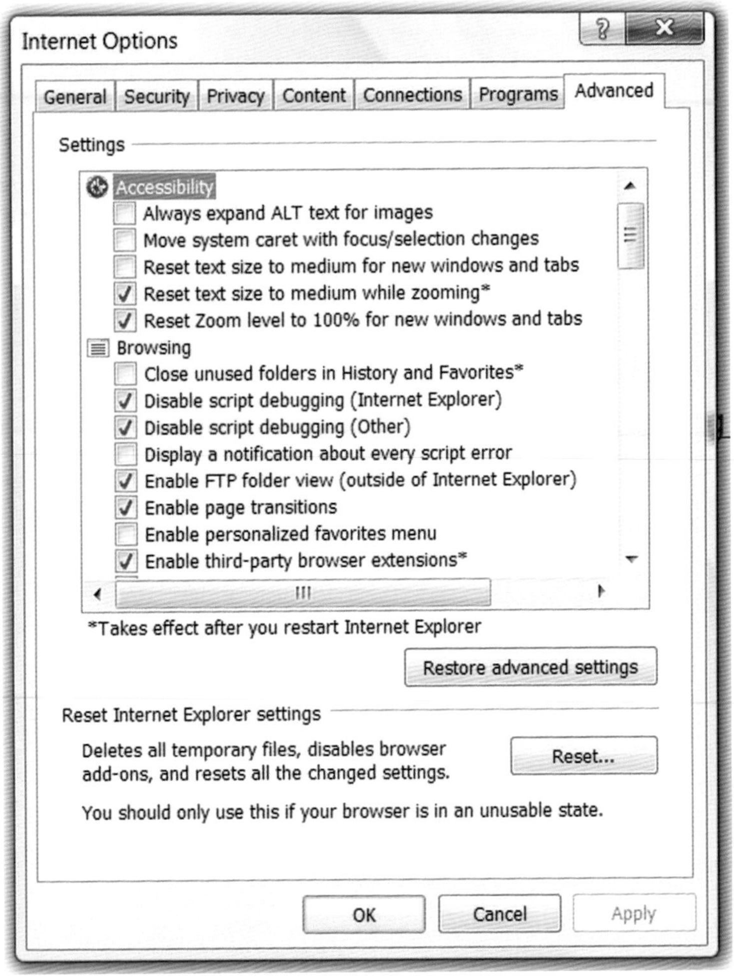

Fig.3.13 Using the Reset button takes Internet Explorer back to its
          original state

the Reset button takes Internet Explorer back to its original state, with no temporary files, no add-ons, and all its original settings.

Something else to try is the built-in diagnosis and repair facility of Windows Vista. This can be accessed by going to the Classic version of the

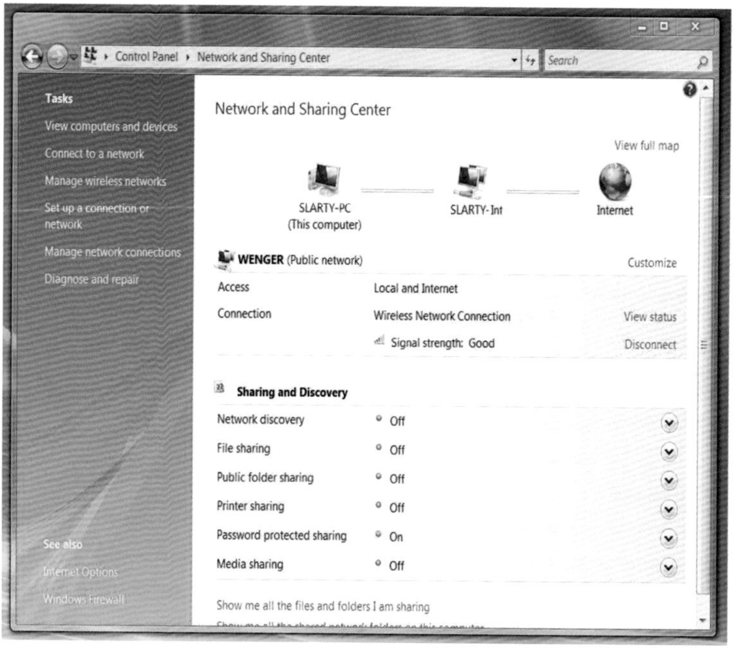

Fig.3.14 Use the "Diagnose and repair" link on the left

Windows Control Panel and double-clicking the Network and Sharing Center icon. The Control Panel window will then change to look something like Figure 3.14, but the network connection or connections shown at the top will reflect the setup of your particular system. In the left-hand panel there is a "Diagnose and repair" link, and left-clicking this gets Windows to look for errors in the connection, and it will also try to repair any that are found.

By this stage things are normally operating properly again, so there is a major problem if the Internet connection is still operating at a snail's pace. One option is to check that the computer is still set up in accordance with your ISP's recommendations. If you were provided with some sort of installation disc when you joined your current ISP it is probably worthwhile running it again. Another option is to use the System Restore facility (see chapter 2) to take the system back to a time when the Internet connection was working at full speed. Where the problem is due to one or more of the system settings being changed, this should certainly undo the changes and get things working normally again.

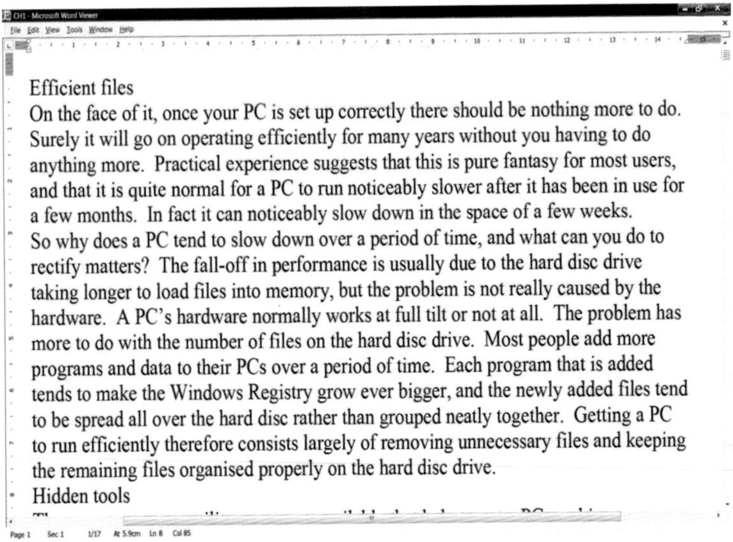

Efficient files
On the face of it, once your PC is set up correctly there should be nothing more to do. Surely it will go on operating efficiently for many years without you having to do anything more. Practical experience suggests that this is pure fantasy for most users, and that it is quite normal for a PC to run noticeably slower after it has been in use for a few months. In fact it can noticeably slow down in the space of a few weeks.
So why does a PC tend to slow down over a period of time, and what can you do to rectify matters? The fall-off in performance is usually due to the hard disc drive taking longer to load files into memory, but the problem is not really caused by the hardware. A PC's hardware normally works at full tilt or not at all. The problem has more to do with the number of files on the hard disc drive. Most people add more programs and data to their PCs over a period of time. Each program that is added tends to make the Windows Registry grow ever bigger, and the newly added files tend to be spread all over the hard disc rather than grouped neatly together. Getting a PC to run efficiently therefore consists largely of removing unnecessary files and keeping the remaining files organised properly on the hard disc drive.
Hidden tools

Fig.3.15 It is not possible to save documents in another format, but they can be copied and pasted into another program

DOC and DOCX files

If someone sends you a document as an Email attachment there is no problem if it is in a general format such as a simple text (txt) file or a rich text format (RTF) type. If you do not have a word processor program that can read these files they can simply be loaded into the Windows WordPad program (Start, All Programs, Accessories, WordPad). Things are a bit more difficult if you are sent DOC or DOCX format files. DOC files are produced by Microsoft's Word program, and DOCX files are the product of the 2007 version of Word. Unfortunately, the built-in WordPad program cannot read either of these file types, although they can be handled by some other word processors.

It is still possible to read these files if your computer is not equipped with a suitable word processor, but it is necessary to download and install Microsoft's Word 2007 Viewer program (Figure 3.15). The installer for this program is just under 25-megabytes in size, so it is within reason even if a dial-up connection is used when downloading it. The installer can be downloaded here:

http://www.microsoft.com/downloads/details.aspx?FamilyId=3657CE88-7CFA-457A-9AEC-F4F827F20CAC&displaylang=en

As its name implies, this is only a viewer program and not a file conversion type. It cannot be used to save files in another format. In fact it has no Save facility at all. Neither does it have any text editing facilities. However, it is possible to use the standard Windows Copy and Paste facilities to transfer material from the viewer program to a word processor such as the built-in WordPad program. The document can then be saved in a standard format such as RTF. Note that it is not necessary to Copy and Paste a document to another program in order to print it. The viewer program has the normal Windows printing facilities.

What scanner?

One of the most common problems with scanners is that users move on to a new version of Windows and then discover that the operating system no longer recognises the scanner. This can actually happen with any item of hardware, and it is simply the result of the old driver software being unsuitable for use with the new version of Windows. In some cases the appropriate driver software will be installed automatically and the problem never arises. In others it is necessary to seek the new driver software from the support section of the manufacturer's web site and then install it manually. With this type of thing it is important to meticulously follow the manufacturer's installation instructions, which should be included on the web site or in a "read.me" file in amongst the downloaded files. Many of these drivers cannot be installed using the standard Windows method.

Of course, manufacturers do not go on providing new driver software for their gadgets until there are none left in working condition. It sometimes becomes necessary to replace a working device because it is not possible to obtain a suitable driver program. The common complaint about scanners is that quite expensive units are often left "high and dry" when they still have plenty of life left in them. Scanner makers and users disagree about the precise interpretation of the word "obsolete". Users quite reasonably feel that a high quality and expensive scanner is not obsolete just because it is a few years old.

There is sometimes a way around this problem in the form of third-party scanning software such as VueScan and SilverFast. These programs usually support a huge range of scanners and several versions of Windows, and in some instances they support a combination of scanner and Windows that the scanner manufacturer does not cater for. The producers of the software write their own drivers when there is nothing suitable available from the maker of the scanner. Some of these programs are available on a trial basis from the usual download sources, so you can check that the software will actually work with your scanner before parting with any money.

Strangely, users often find that their original scanning software suddenly becomes usable again once a third party scanning program has been installed on the computer. Presumably the driver software included with the scanning program is standard Windows type that installs the scanner into Windows in the normal way. The scanner is then available for use with any program that can use a scanner. You then have the option of returning to the old scanning software or using the new program. Of course, you should still pay for the new software even if you revert to the original scanning program, because you will still be using part of the new software package.

Index